A NONSENSE ANTHOLOGY

HE must be a fool indeed who cannot at times play the fool; and he who does not enjoy nonsense must be lacking in sense.

WILLIAM J. ROLFE.

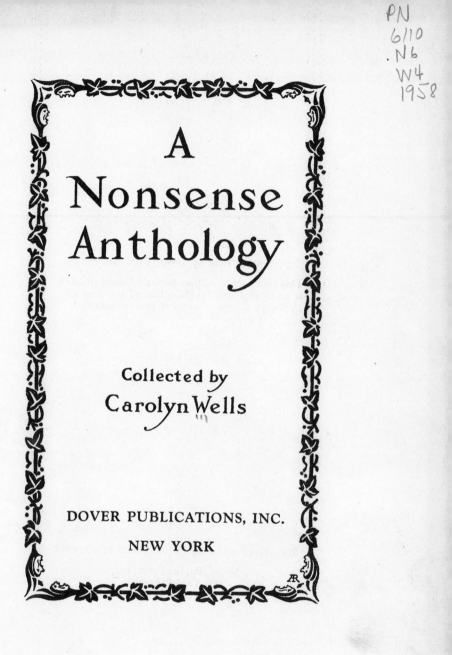

A Nonsense Anthology

Collected by

Carolyn Wells

DOVER PUBLICATIONS, INC.

NEW YORK

Manufactured in the United States of America

Dover Publications, Inc.
180 Varick Street
New York 14, N. Y.

TO

GELETT BURGESS

A NONSENSE LOVER

CONTENTS

[vii]

Contents

"SERIOUS" SUBJECTS

HIGH SENTIMENTS

Contents

[ix]

Contents

[x]

Contents

[xi]

Contents

[xii]

Contents

[xiii]

Contents

Contents

[xv]

Contents

INTRODUCTION

INTRODUCTION

ON a topographical map of Literature Nonsense would be represented by a small and sparsely settled country, neglected by the average tourist, but affording keen delight to the few enlightened travellers who sojourn within its borders. It is a field which has been neglected by anthologists and essayists; one of its few serious recognitions being in a certain " Treatise of Figurative Language," which says : " Nonsense ; shall we dignify that with a place on our list ? Assuredly will vote for doing so every one who hath at all duly noticed what admirable and wise uses it can be, and often is, put to, though never before in rhetoric has it been so highly honored. How deeply does clever or quaint nonsense abide in the memory, and for how many a decade — from earliest youth to age's most venerable years."

And yet Hazlitt's " Studies in Jocular Literature " mentions six divisions of the Jest, and omits Nonsense !

Perhaps, partly because of such neglect, the work of the best nonsense writers is less widely known than it might be.

But a more probable reason is that the majority of the reading world does not appreciate or enjoy real nonsense, and this, again, is consequent upon their inability to discriminate between nonsense of integral merit and simple chaff.

> A jest's prosperity lies in the ear
> Of him that hears it.   Never in the tongue
> Of him that makes it,

and a sense of nonsense is as distinct a part of our mentality as a sense of humor, being by no means identical therewith.

It is a fad at present for a man to relate a nonsensical story, and then, if his hearer does not laugh, say gravely : "You have no sense of humor. That is a test story, and only a true humorist laughs at it." Now, the hearer may have an exquisite sense of humor, but he may be lacking in a sense of nonsense, and so the story gives him no pleasure.   De Quincey said, "None but a man of extraordinary talent can write first-rate nonsense." Only a short study of the subject is required to convince us that De Quincey was right ; and he might have added, none but a man of extraordinary taste can appreciate first-rate nonsense.   As an instance of this, we may remember that Edward Lear, "the parent of modern nonsense-writers," was a talented author and artist, and a prime favorite of such men as Tennyson and the Earls of

---

Derby; and John Ruskin placed Lear's name at the head of his list of the best hundred authors.

"Don't tell me," said William Pitt, "of a man's being able to talk sense; every one can talk sense. Can he talk nonsense?"

The sense of nonsense enables us not only to discern pure nonsense, but to consider intelligently nonsense of various degrees of purity. Absence of sense is not necessarily nonsense, any more than absence of justice is injustice.

Etymologically speaking, nonsense may be either words without meaning, or words conveying absurd or ridiculous ideas. It is the second definition which expresses the great mass of nonsense literature, but there is a small proportion of written nonsense which comes under the head of language without meaning.

Again, there are verses composed entirely of meaningless words, which are not nonsense literature, because they are written with some other intent.

The nursery rhyme, of which there are almost as many versions as there are nurseries,

> Eena, meena, mona, mi,
> Bassalona, bona, stri,
> Hare, ware, frown, whack,
> Halico balico, we, wi, wo, wack,

is not strictly a nonsense verse, because it was invented and used for "counting out," and the arbitrary words simply take the place of the numbers 1, 2, 3, etc.

Also, the nonsense verses with which students of Latin composition are sometimes taught to begin their efforts, where words are used with no relative meaning, simply to familiarize the pupil with the mechanical values of quantity and metre, are not nonsense. It is only nonsense for nonsense' sake that is now under our consideration.

Doubtless the best and best-known example of versified words without meaning is " Jabberwocky." Although (notwithstanding Lewis Carroll's explanations) the coined words are absolutely without meaning, the rhythm is perfect and the poetic quality decidedly apparent, and the poem appeals to the nonsense lover as a work of pure genius. Bayard Taylor is said to have recited " Jabberwocky " aloud for his own delectation until he was forced to stop by uncontrollable laughter. To us who know our *Alice* it would seem unnecessary to quote this poem, but it is a fact that among the general reading community the appreciators of Lewis Carroll are surprisingly few. An editor of a leading literary review, when asked recently if he had read " Alice in Wonderland," replied, " No, but I mean to. It is by the author of ' As in a Looking-Glass,' is it not ? "

But of far greater interest and merit than nonsense of words, is nonsense of ideas. Here, again, we distinguish between nonsense and no sense. Ideas conveying no sense are often intensely funny, and this type is seen in some of the best of our nonsense literature.

A perfect specimen is the bit of evidence read by the White Rabbit at the Trial of the Knave of Hearts.[1] One charm of these verses is the serious air of legal directness which pervades their ambiguity, and another is the precision with which the metrical accent coincides exactly with the natural emphasis. They are marked, too, by the liquid euphony that always distinguishes Lewis Carroll's poetry.

A different type is found in verses that refer to objects in terms the opposite of true, thereby suggesting ludicrous incongruity, and there is also the nonsense verse that uses word effects which have been confiscated by the poets and tacitly given over to them.

A refrain of nonsense words is a favorite diversion of many otherwise serious poets.

With a hey, and a ho, and a hey nonino,

is one of Shakespeare's many musical nonsense refrains.

1 " She 's all my Fancy painted him," page 20.

Burns gives us :

> Ken ye aught o' Captain Grose ?
> Igo and ago,
> If he 's 'mang his freens or foes ?
> Iram, coram, dago.
> Is he slain by Highlan' bodies ?
> Igo and ago ;
> And eaten like a weather haggis ?
> Iram, coram, dago.

Another very old refrain runs thus :

> Rorum, corum, sunt di-vorum,
> Harum, scarum, divo;
> Tag-rag, merry-derry, periwig and hat-band,
> Hic, hoc, horum, genitivo.

An old ballad written before the Reformation has for a refrain :

> Sing go trix,
> Trim go trix,
> Under the greenwood tree.

While a celebrated political ballad is known by its nonsense chorus,

> Lilliburlero bullin a-la.

Mother Goose rhymes abound in these nonsense refrains, and they are often fine examples of onomatopœia.

By far the most meritorious and most interesting kind of nonsense is that which embodies an absurd or ridiculous idea, and treats it with elaborate seriousness. The greatest masters of this art are undoubtedly Edward Lear and Lewis Carroll. These Englishmen were men of genius, deep thinkers, and hard workers.

Lear was an artist draughtsman, his subjects being mainly ornithological and zoölogical. Lewis Carroll (Charles L. Dodgson) was an expert in mathematics and a lecturer on that science in Christ Church, Oxford.

Both these men numbered among their friends many of the greatest Englishmen of the day. Tennyson was a warm friend and admirer of each, as was also John Ruskin.

Lear's first nonsense verses, published in 1846, are written in the form of the well-known stanza beginning :

> There was an old man of Tobago.

This type of stanza, known as the "Limerick," is said by a gentleman who speaks with authority to have flourished in the reign of William IV. This is one of several he remembers as current at his public school in 1834:

> There was a young man at St. Kitts
> Who was very much troubled with fits ;
> The eclipse of the moon
> Threw him into a swoon,
> When he tumbled and broke into bits.

Lear distinctly asserts that this form of verse was not invented by him, but was suggested by a friend as a useful model for amusing rhymes. It proved so in his case, for he published no less than two hundred and twelve of these " Limericks."

In regard to his verses, Lear asserted that " nonsense, pure and absolute," was his aim throughout; and remarked, further, that to have been the means of administering innocent mirth to thousands was surely a just excuse for satisfaction. He pursued his aim with scrupulous consistency, and his absurd conceits are fantastic and ridiculous, but never cheaply or vulgarly funny.

Twenty-five years after his first book came out, Lear published other books of nonsense verse and prose, with pictures which are irresistibly mirth-provoking. Lear's nonsense songs, while retaining all the ludicrous merriment of his Limericks, have an added quality of poetic harmony. They are distinctly *singable*, and many of them have been set to music by talented composers. Perhaps the best-known songs are " The Owl and the Pussy-Cat " and " The Daddy-Long-Legs and the Fly."

Lear himself composed airs for " The Pelican Chorus " and " The Yonghy-Bonghy Bò," which were arranged for the piano by Professor Pomè, of San Remo, Italy.

Although like Lear's in some respects, Lewis Carroll's nonsense is perhaps of a more refined type. There is less of the grotesque and more poetic imagery. But though Carroll was more of a poet than Lear, both had the true sense of nonsense. Both assumed the most absurd conditions, and proceeded to detail their consequences with a simple seriousness that convulses appreciative readers, and we find ourselves uncertain whether it is the manner or the matter that is more amusing.

Lewis Carroll was a man of intellect and education; his funniest sayings are often based on profound knowledge or deep thought. Like Lear, he never spoiled his quaint fancies by over-exaggerating their quaintness or their fancifulness, and his ridiculous plots are as carefully conceived, constructed, and elaborated as though they embodied the soundest facts. No funny detail is ever allowed to become *too* funny; and it is in this judicious economy of extravagance that his genius is shown. As he remarks in one of his own poems:

> Then, fourthly, there are epithets
> That suit with any word —
> As well as Harvey's Reading Sauce
> With fish, or flesh, or bird.

. . . . . .

Such epithets, like pepper,
Give zest to what you write;
And, if you strew them sparely,
They whet the appetite;
But if you lay them on too thick,
You spoil the matter quite!

Both Lear and Carroll suffered from the undiscerning critics who persisted in seeing in their nonsense a hidden meaning, a cynical, political, or other intent, veiled under the apparent foolery. Lear takes occasion to deny this in the preface to one of his books, and asserts not only that his rhymes and pictures have no symbolical meaning, but that he "took more care than might be supposed to make the subjects incapable of such misinterpretation."

Likewise, "Jabberwocky" was declared by one critic to be a translation from the German, and by others its originality was doubted. The truth is, that it was written by Lewis Carroll at an evening party; it was quite impromptu, and no ulterior meaning was intended. "The Hunting of the Snark" was also regarded by some as an allegory, or, perhaps, a burlesque on a celebrated case, in which the *Snark* was used as a personification of popularity, but Lewis Carroll protested that the poem had no meaning at all.

A favorite trick of the Nonsensists is the coining

of words to suit their needs, and Lear and Carroll are especially happy in their inventions of this kind.

Lear gives us such gems as scroobious, meloobious, ombliferous, borascible, slobaciously, himmeltanious, flumpetty, and mumbian; while the best of Lewis Carroll's coined words are those found in " Jabberwocky."

Another of the great Nonsensists is W. S. Gilbert. Unlike Lear or Carroll, his work is not characterized by absurd words or phrases; he prefers a still wider scope, and invents a ridiculous plot. The " Bab Ballads," as well as Mr. Gilbert's comic opera librettos, hinge upon schemes of ludicrous impossibility, which are treated as the most natural proceedings in the world. The best known of the " Bab Ballads " is no doubt " The Yarn of the 'Nancy Bell,' " which was long since set to music and is still a popular song. In addition to his talent for nonsense, Mr. Gilbert possesses a wonderful rhyming facility, and juggles cleverly with difficult and unusual metres.

In regard to his " Bab Ballads," Mr. Gilbert gravely says that " they are not, as a rule, founded on fact," and, remembering their gory and often cannibalistic tendencies, we are grateful for this assurance. An instance of Gilbert's appreciation of other people's nonsense is his parody of Lear's verse :

There was an old man in a tree
Who was horribly bored by a bee ;
    When they said, " Does it buzz ? "
    He replied, " Yes, it does !
It 's a regular brute of a bee ! "

The parody attributed to Gilbert is called " A Nonsense Rhyme in Blank Verse " :

There was an old man of St. Bees,
Who was stung in the arm by a wasp ;
    When they asked, " Does it hurt ? "
    He replied, " No, it does n't,
But I thought all the while 't was a Hornet ! "

Thackeray wrote spirited nonsense, but much of it had an under-meaning, political or otherwise, which bars it from the field of sheer nonsense.

The sense of nonsense is no respecter of persons ; even staid old Dr. Johnson possessed it, though his nonsense verses are marked by credible fact and irrefutable logic. Witness these two examples :

As with my hat upon my head
    I walked along the Strand,
I there did meet another man
    With his hat in his hand.

The tender infant, meek and mild,
    Fell down upon the stone ;
The nurse took up the squealing child,
    But still the child squealed on.

[xxx]

The Doctor is also responsible for

> If a man who turnips cries,
> Cry not when his father dies,
> 'T is a proof that he would rather
> Have a turnip than a father.

And indeed, among our best writers there are few who have not dropped into nonsense or semi-nonsense at one time or another.

A familiar bit of nonsense prose is by S. Foote, and it is said that Charles Macklin used to recite it with great gusto :

" She went into the garden to cut a cabbage-leaf to make an apple-pie, and at the same time a great she-bear coming up the street, pops its head into the shop. ' What, no soap ? ' so he died. She imprudently married the barber, and there were present the Pickaninnies, the Joblilies, the Gayrulies, and the Grand Panjandrum himself with the little round button on top, and they all fell to playing catch-as-catch-can till the gunpowder ran out at the heels of their boots."

An old nonsense verse attributed to an Oxford student, is the well known

> A centipede was happy quite,
> Until a frog in fun
> Said, " Pray, which leg comes after which ? "
> This raised her mind to such a pitch,
> She lay distracted in the ditch
> Considering how to run.

So far as we know, Kipling has never printed

anything which can be called nonsense verse, but it is doubtless only a question of time when that branch shall be added to his versatility. His "Just So" stories are capital nonsense prose, and the following rhyme proves him guilty of at least one Limerick :

> There was a small boy of Quebec,
> Who was buried in snow to his neck ;
> When they said, " Are you friz ? "
> He replied, " Yes, I is —
> But we don't call this cold in Quebec."

Among living authors, one who has written a great amount of good nonsense is Mr. Gelett Burgess, late editor of *The Lark*.

According to Mr. Burgess' own statement, the test of nonsense is its quotability, and his work stands this test admirably, for what absurd rhyme ever attained such popularity as his "Purple Cow"? This was first printed in *The Lark*, a paper published in San Francisco for two years, the only periodical of any merit that has ever made intelligent nonsense its special feature.

Another of the most talented nonsense writers of to-day is Mr. Oliver Herford. It is a pity, however, to reproduce his verse without his illustrations, for as nonsense these are as admirable as the text. But the greater part of Mr. Herford's work belongs to the realm of pure fancy, and though of a whimsical delicacy often equal to Lewis Carroll's, it is rarely sheer nonsense.

As a proof that good nonsense is by no means an easy achievement, attention is called to a recent competition inaugurated by the London *Academy*.

Nonsense rhymes similar to those quoted from *The Lark* were asked for, and though many were received, it is stated that no brilliant results were among them.

The prize was awarded to this weak and uninteresting specimen:

> " If half the road was made of jam,
>   The other half of bread,
> How very nice my walks would be,"
>   The greedy infant said.

These two were also offered by competitors:

> I love to stand upon my head
>   And think of things sublime
> Until my mother interrupts
>   And says it's dinner-time.

> A lobster wooed a lady crab,
>   And kissed her lovely face.
> " Upon my sole," the crabbess cried,
>   " I wish you 'd mind your plaice ! "

Let us, then, give Nonsense its place among the divisions of Humor, and though we cannot reduce it to an exact science, let us acknowledge it as a fine art.

A NONSENSE ANTHOLOGY

A Nonsense Anthology

JABBERWOCKY

'TWAS brillig, and the slithy toves
    Did gyre and gimble in the wabe;
    All mimsy were the borogoves,
And the mome raths outgrabe.

" Beware the Jabberwock, my son !
    The jaws that bite, the claws that catch !
Beware the Jubjub bird, and shun
    The frumious Bandersnatch ! "

He took his vorpal sword in hand :
    Long time the manxome foe he sought.
So rested he by the Tumtum tree,
    And stood awhile in thought.

And as in uffish thought he stood,
    The Jabberwock with eyes of flame,
Came whiffling through the tulgey wood,
    And burbled as it came !

One, two ! One, two ! And through, and through
    The vorpal blade went snicker-snack !
He left it dead, and with its head
    He went galumphing back.

"And hast thou slain the Jabberwock?
Come to my arms, my beamish boy!
Oh, frabjous day! Callooh! callay!"
He chortled in his joy.

'T was brillig, and the slithy toves
Did gyre and gimble in the wabe;
All mimsy were the borogoves
And the mome raths outgrabe.

Lewis Carroll.

MORS IABROCHII

C ŒSPER [1] erat: tunc lubriciles [2] ultravia
circum
Urgebant gyros gimbiculosque tophi;
Mœstenui visæ borogovides ire meatu;
Et profugi gemitus exgrabuêre rathæ.

O fuge Iabrochium, sanguis meus! [3] Ille recurvis
Unguibus, estque avidis dentibus ille minax.
Ububæ fuge cautus avis vim, gnate! Neque
unquam
Fæderpax contra te frumiosus eat!

[1] *Cœsper* from *Cœna* and *vesper.*
[2] *lubriciles* from *lubricus* and *graciles.* See the Commentary in Humpty Dumpty's square, which will also explain *ultravia,* and — if it requires explanation — *mœstenui.*
[3] *Sanguis meus:* cf. Verg. Æn. 6. 836,
"Projice tela manu, sanguis meus!"

Vorpali gladio juvenis succingitur : hostis
  Manxumus ad medium quæritur usque diem :
Jamque viâ fesso, sed plurima mente prementi,
  Tumtumiæ frondis suaserat umbra moram.

Consilia interdum stetit egnia [1] mene revolvens ;
  At gravis in densâ fronde susuffrus [2] erat,
Spiculaque [3] ex oculis jacientis flammea, tulseam
  Per silvam venit burbur [4] Iabrochii !

Vorpali, semel atque iterum collectus in ictum,
  Persnicuit gladis persnacuitque puer :
Deinde galumphatus, spernens informe Cadaver,
  Horrendum monstri rettulit ipse caput.

Victor Iabrochii, spoliis insignis opimis,
  Rursus in amplexus, o radiose, meos !
O frabiose dies ! CALLO clamateque CALLA !
  Vix potuit lætus chorticulare pater.

Cœsper erat : tunc lubriciles ultravia circum
  Urgebant gyros gimbiculosque tophi ;
Mœstenui visæ borogovides ire meatu ;
  Et profugi gemitus exgrabuêre rathæ.

Anonymous.

[1] *egnia :* " muffish "= segnis ; . . . " uffish "= egnis. This
is a conjectural analogy, but I can suggest no better solution.
[2] *susuffrus :* " whiffling " : : *susurrus :* " whistling."
[3] *spicula :* see the picture.
[4] *burbur :* apparently a labial variation of *murmur*,
stronger but more dissonant.

[5]

THE NYUM-NYUM

THE Nyum-Nyum chortled by the sea,
    And sipped the wavelets green :
    He wondered how the sky could be
So very nice and clean ;

He wondered if the chambermaid
    Had swept the dust away,
And if the scrumptious Jabberwock
    Had mopped it up that day.

And then in sadness to his love
    The Nyum-Nyum weeping said,
I know no reason why the sea
    Should not be white or red.

I know no reason why the sea
    Should not be red, I say ;
And why the slithy Bandersnatch
    Has not been round to-day.

He swore he 'd call at two o'clock,
    And now it 's half-past four.
" Stay," said the Nyum-Nyum's love, " I think
    I hear him at the door."

In twenty minutes in there came
    A creature black as ink,
Which put its feet upon a chair
    And called for beer to drink.

[6]

They gave him porter in a tub,
  But, " Give me more ! " he cried ;
And then he drew a heavy sigh,
  And laid him down, and died.

He died, and in the Nyum-Nyum's cave
  A cry of mourning rose ;
The Nyum-Nyum sobbed a gentle sob,
  And slily blew his nose.

The Nyum-Nyum's love, we need not state,
  Was overwhelmed and sad ;
She said, " Oh, take the corpse away,
  Or you will drive me mad ! "

The Nyum-Nyum in his supple arms
  Took up the gruesome weight,
And, with a cry of bitter fear,
  He threw it at his mate.

And then he wept, and tore his hair,
  And threw it in the sea,
And loudly sobbed with streaming eyes
  That such a thing could be.

The ox, that mumbled in his stall,
  Perspired and gently sighed,
And then, in sympathy, it fell
  Upon its back and died.

The hen that sat upon her eggs,
  With high ambition fired,
Arose in simple majesty,
  And, with a cluck, expired.

The jubejube bird, that carolled there,
  Sat down upon a post,
And with a reverential caw,
  Gave up its little ghost.

And ere its kind and loving life
  Eternally had ceased,
The donkey, in the ancient barn,
  In agony deceased.

The raven, perched upon the elm,
  Gave forth a scraping note,
And ere the sound had died away,
  Had cut its tuneful throat.

The Nyum-Nyum's love was sorrowful;
  And, after she had cried,
She, with a brand-new carving-knife,
  Committed suicide.

"Alas!" the Nyum-Nyum said, "alas!
  With thee I will not part,"
And straightway seized a rolling-pin
  And drove it through his heart.

[8]

The mourners came and gathered up
    The bits that lay about;
But why the massacre had been,
    They could not quite make out.

One said there was a mystery
    Connected with the deaths;
But others thought the silent ones
    Perhaps had lost their breaths.

The doctor soon arrived, and viewed
    The corpses as they lay;
He could not give them life again,
    So he was heard to say.

But, oh! it was a horrid sight;
    It made the blood run cold,
To see the bodies carried off
    And covered up with mould.

The Toves across the briny sea
    Wept buckets-full of tears;
They were relations of the dead,
    And had been friends for years.

The Jabberwock upon the hill
    Gave forth a gloomy wail,
When in his airy seat he sat,
    And told the awful tale.

And who can wonder that it made
That loving creature cry?
For he had done the dreadful work
And caused the things to die.

That Jabberwock was passing bad —
That Jabberwock was wrong,
And with this verdict I conclude
One portion of my song.

Anonymous.

UFFIA

WHEN sporgles spanned the floreate mead
And cogwogs gleet upon the lea,
Uffia gopped to meet her love
Who smeeged upon the equat sea.

Dately she walked aglost the sand;
The boreal wind seet in her face;
The moggling waves yalped at her feet;
Pangwangling was her pace.

Harriet R. White.

SPIRK TROLL–DERISIVE *

THE Crankadox leaned o'er the edge of the
moon,
And wistfully gazed on the sea
Where the Gryxabodill madly whistled a tune
To the air of "Ti-fol-de-ding-dee."

* By permission of the author; from " Spirk and Wunk Rhymes,"
copyright, 1891, 1898.

The quavering shriek of the Fliupthecreek
  Was fitfully wafted afar
To the Queen of the Wunks as she powdered her
    cheek
  With the pulverized rays of a star.

The Gool closed his ear on the voice of the
    Grig,
  And his heart it grew heavy as lead
As he marked the Baldekin adjusting his wig
  On the opposite side of his head ;
And the air it grew chill as the Gryxabodill
  Raised his dank, dripping fins to the skies
To plead with the Plunk for the use of her bill
  To pick the tears out of his eyes.

The ghost of the Zhack flitted by in a trance;
  And the Squidjum hid under a tub
As he heard the loud hooves of the Hooken
    advance
  With a rub-a-dub-dub-a-dub dub !
And the Crankadox cried as he laid down and died,
  " My fate there is none to bewail ! "
While the Queen of the Wunks drifted over the
    tide
  With a long piece of crape to her tail.

                James Whitcomb Riley.

THE WHANGO TREE

THE woggly bird sat on the whango tree,
   Nooping the rinkum corn,
  And graper and graper, alas ! grew he,
And cursed the day he was born.
His crute was clum and his voice was rum,
  As curiously thus sang he,
" Oh, would I'd been rammed and eternally
    clammed
  Ere I perched on this whango tree."

Now the whango tree had a bubbly thorn,
  As sharp as a nootie's bill,
And it stuck in the woggly bird's umptum lorn
  And weepadge, the smart did thrill.
He fumbled and cursed, but that was n't the worst,
  For he could n't at all get free,
And he cried, " I am gammed, and injustibly
    nammed
  On the luggardly whango tree."

And there he sits still, with no worm in his bill,
  Nor no guggledom in his nest;
He is hungry and bare, and gobliddered with care,
  And his grabbles give him no rest;
He is weary and sore and his tugmut is soar,
  And nothing to nob has he,
As he chirps, " I am blammed and corruptibly
    jammed,
  In this cuggerdom whango tree."   *1840.*

SING FOR THE GARISH EYE

SING for the garish eye,
    When moonless brandlings cling !
    Let the froddering crooner cry,
And the braddled sapster sing.
For never and never again,
    Will the tottering beechlings play,
For bratticed wrackers are singing aloud,
    And the throngers croon in May !

W. S. Gilbert.

THE CRUISE OF THE "P. C."

ACROSS the swiffling waves they went,
    The gumly bark yoked to and fro;
    The jupple crew on pleasure bent,
Galored, " This is a go ! "

Beside the poo's'l stood the Gom,
    He chirked and murgled in his glee;
While near him, in a grue jipon,
    The Bard was quite at sea.

" Gollop ! Golloy ! Thou scrumjous Bard !
    Take pen (thy stylo) and endite
A pome, my brain needs kurgling hard,
    And I will feast tonight."

[13]

That wansome Bard he took his pen,
   A flirgly look around he guv;
He squoffled once, he squirled, and then
   He wrote what's writ above.

Anonymous.

TO MARIE

WHEN the breeze from the bluebottle's blus-
        tering blim
     Twirls the toads in a tooroomaloo,
And the whiskery whine of the wheedlesome
    whim
   Drowns the roll of the rattatattoo,
Then I dream in the shade of the shally-go-shee,
   And the voice of the bally-molay
Brings the smell of the pale poppy-cod's blum-
    mered blee
   From the willy-wad over the way.

Ah, the shuddering shoe and the blinketty-blanks
   When the punglung falls from the bough
In the blast of a hurricane's hicketty-hanks
   O'er the hills of the hocketty-how!
Give the rigamarole to the clangery-whang,
   If they care for such fiddlededee;
But the thingumbob kiss of the whangery-bang
   Keeps the higgledy-piggle for me.

L'ENVOI

It is pilly-po-doddle and aligobung
  When the lollypup covers the ground,
Yet the poldiddle perishes plunkety-pung
  When the heart jimny-coggles around.
If the soul cannot snoop at the gigglesome cart
  Seeking surcease in gluggety-glug,
It is useless to say to the pulsating heart,
  " Yankee-doodle ker-chuggety-chug ! "

Anonymous.

LUNAR STANZAS

NIGHT saw the crew like pedlers with their
      packs
    Altho' it were too dear to pay for eggs ;
Walk crank along with coffin on their backs
While in their arms they bow their weary legs.

And yet 't was strange, and scarce can one suppose
  That a brown buzzard-fly should steal and wear
His white jean breeches and black woollen hose,
But thence that flies have souls is very clear.

But, Holy Father ! what shall save the soul,
  When cobblers ask three dollars for their shoes ?
When cooks their biscuits with a shot-tower roll,
  And farmers rake their hay-cocks with their
    hoes.

Yet, 't were profuse to see for pendant light,
  A tea-pot dangle in a lady's ear;
And 't were indelicate, although she might
  Swallow two whales and yet the moon shine
    clear.

But what to me are woven clouds, or what,
  If dames from spiders learn to warp their looms?
If coal-black ghosts turn soldiers for the State,
  With wooden eyes, and lightning-rods for
    plumes?

Oh! too, too shocking! barbarous, savage taste!
  To eat one's mother ere itself was born!
To gripe the tall town-steeple by the waste,
  And scoop it out to be his drinking-horn.

No more: no more!   I 'm sick and dead and gone;
  Boxed in a coffin, stifled six feet deep;
Thorns, fat and fearless, prick my skin and bone,
  And revel o'er me, like a soulless sheep.

Henry Coggswell Knight, 1815.

NONSENSE

OH that my Lungs could bleat like butter'd
    Pease;
    But bleating of my lungs hath Caught the
    itch,
And are as mangy as the Irish Seas
  That offer wary windmills to the Rich.

I grant that Rainbowes being lull'd asleep,
    Snort like a woodknife in a Lady's eyes ;
Which makes her grieve to see a pudding creep,
    For Creeping puddings only please the wise.

Not that a hard-row'd herring should presume
    To swing a tyth pig in a Cateskin purse ;
For fear the hailstons which did fall at Rome,
    By lesning of the fault should make it worse.

For 't is most certain Winter woolsacks grow
    From geese to swans if men could keep them so,
Till that the sheep shorn Planets gave the hint
    To pickle pancakes in Geneva print.

Some men there were that did suppose the skie
    Was made of Carbonado'd Antidotes ;
But my opinion is, a Whale's left eye,
    Need not be coynéd all King Harry groates.

The reason's plain, for Charon's Westerne barge
    Running a tilt at the Subjunctive mood,
Beckoned to Bednal Green, and gave him charge
    To fasten padlockes with Antartic food.

The End will be the Mill ponds must be laded,
    To fish for white pots in a Country dance ;
So they that suffered wrong and were upbraded
    Shall be made friends in a left-handed trance.

Anonymous, 1617.

SONNET FOUND IN A DESERTED MAD HOUSE

OH that my soul a marrow-bone might seize!
  For the old egg of my desire is broken,
  Spilled is the pearly white and spilled the yolk, and
As the mild melancholy contents grease
My path the shorn lamb baas like bumblebees.
Time's trashy purse is as a taken token
Or like a thrilling recitation, spoken
By mournful mouths filled full of mirth and cheese.

And yet, why should I clasp the earthful urn?
Or find the frittered fig that felt the fast?
Or choose to chase the cheese around the churn?
Or swallow any pill from out the past?
Ah, no Love, not while your hot kisses burn
Like a potato riding on the blast.

Anonymous.

THE OCEAN WANDERER

BRIGHT breaks the warrior o'er the ocean wave
  Through realms that rove not, clouds that cannot save,
Sinks in the sunshine; dazzles o'er the tomb
And mocks the mutiny of Memory's gloom.

[18]

Oh! who can feel the crimson ecstasy
That soothes with bickering jar the Glorious
Tree?
O'er the high rock the foam of gladness throws,
While star-beams lull Vesuvius to repose:
Girds the white spray, and in the blue lagoon,
Weeps like a walrus o'er the waning moon?
Who can declare? — not thou, pervading boy
Whom pibrochs pierce not, crystals cannot cloy; —
Not thou soft Architect of silvery gleams,
Whose soul would simmer in Hesperian streams,
Th' exhaustless fire — the bosom's azure bliss,
That hurtles, life-like, o'er a scene like this; —
Defies the distant agony of Day —
And sweeps o'er hetacombs — away! away!
Say shall Destruction's lava load the gale,
The furnace quiver and the mountain quail?
Say shall the son of Sympathy pretend
His cedar fragrance with our Chief's to blend?
There, where the gnarled monuments of sand
Howl their dark whirlwinds to the levin brand;
Conclusive tenderness; fraternal grog,
Tidy conjunction; adamantine bog,
Impetuous arrant toadstool; Thundering quince,
Repentant dog-star, inessential Prince,
Expound. Pre-Adamite eventful gun,
Crush retribution, currant-jelly, pun,
Oh! eligible Darkness, fender, sting,
Heav'n-born Insanity, courageous thing.
Intending, bending, scouring, piercing all,
Death like pomatum, tea, and crabs must fall.

Anonymous.

[19]

SHE'S ALL MY FANCY PAINTED
HIM

SHE's all my fancy painted him,
   (I make no idle boast);
  If he or you had lost a limb,
   Which would have suffered most?

He said that you had been to her,
   And seen me here before:
But, in another character
   She was the same of yore.

There was not one that spoke to us,
   Of all that thronged the street;
So he sadly got into a 'bus,
   And pattered with his feet.

They told me you had been to her,
   And mentioned me to him;
She gave me a good character,
   But said I could not swim.

He sent them word I had not gone
   (We know it to be true);
If she should push the matter on,
   What would become of you?

I gave her one, they gave him two,
   You gave us three or more;
They all returned from him to you,
   Though they were mine before.

If I or she should chance to be
   Involved in this affair,
He trusts to you to set them free,
   Exactly as we were.

My notion was that you had been
   (Before she had this fit)
An obstacle that came between
   Him, and ourselves, and it.

Don't let him know she liked them best,
   For this must ever be
A secret, kept from all the rest,
   Between yourself and me.

Lewis Carroll.

MY RECOLLECTEST THOUGHTS *

MY recollectest thoughts are those
   Which I remember yet;
And bearing on, as you 'd suppose,
   The things I don't forget.

* By permission of the author; from "Davy and the Goblin,"
copyright, 1884, 1885, by The Century Co.; 1885, by Ticknor
& Co.

But my resemblest thoughts are less
    Alike than they should be ;
A state of things, as you 'll confess,
    You very seldom see.

And yet the mostest thought I love
    Is what no one believes —
That I 'm the sole survivor of
    The famous Forty Thieves !

                       Charles E. Carryl.

FATHER WILLIAM

YOU are old, Father William," the young
      man said,
    " And your nose has a look of surprise ;
Your eyes have turned round to the back of your
    head,
    And you live upon cucumber pies."
" I know it, I know it," the old man replied,
    " And it comes from employing a quack,
Who said if I laughed when the crocodile died
    I should never have pains in my back."

" You are old, Father William," the young man
    said,
    " And your legs always get in your way ;
You use too much mortar in mixing your bread,
    And you try to drink timothy hay."

" Very true, very true," said the wretched old man,
" Every word that you tell me is true ;
And it 's caused by my having my kerosene can
Painted red where it ought to be blue."

"You are old, Father William," the young man
said,
" And your teeth are beginning to freeze,
Your favorite daughter has wheels in her head,
And the chickens are eating your knees."
" You are right," said the old man, " I cannot deny,
That my troubles are many and great,
But I 'll butter my ears on the Fourth of July,
And then I 'll be able to skate."

Anonymous.

IN THE GLOAMING

THE twilight twiles in the vernal vale,
In adumbration of azure awe,
And I listlessly list in my swallow-tail
To the limpet licking his limber jaw.
And it 's O for the sound of the daffodil,
For the dry distillings of prawn and prout,
When hope hops high and a heather hill
Is a dear delight and a darksome doubt.
The snagwap sits in the bosky brae
And sings to the gumplet in accents sweet ;
The gibwink has n't a word to say,
But pensively smiles at the fair keeweet.

[23]

And it 's O for the jungles of Boorabul.
　For the jingling jungles to jangle in,
With a moony maze of mellado mull,
　And a protoplasm for next of kin.
O, sweet is the note of the shagreen shard
　And mellow the mew of the mastodon,
When the soboliferous Somminard
　Is scenting the shadows at set of sun.
And it 's O for the timorous tamarind
　In the murky meadows of Mariboo,
For the suave sirocco of Sazerkind,
　And the pimpernell pellets of Pangipoo.

James C. Bayles.

BALLAD OF BEDLAM

OH, lady, wake! the azure moon
　　Is rippling in the verdant skies,
　　The owl is warbling his soft tune,
　Awaiting but thy snowy eyes.
The joys of future years are past,
　To-morrow's hopes have fled away ;
Still let us love, and e'en at last
　We shall be happy yesterday.

The early beam of rosy night
　Drives off the ebon morn afar,
While through the murmur of the light
　The huntsman winds his mad guitar.

Then, lady, wake! my brigantine
Pants, neighs, and prances to be free;
Till the creation I am thine,
To some rich desert fly with me.

Punch.

'T IS SWEET TO ROAM

'TIS sweet to roam when morning's light
Resounds across the deep;
And the crystal song of the woodbine
bright
Hushes the rocks to sleep,
And the blood-red moon in the blaze of noon
Is bathed in a crumbling dew,
And the wolf rings out with a glittering shout,
To-whit, to-whit, to-whoo!

Anonymous.

HYMN TO THE SUNRISE

THE dreamy crags with raucous voices croon
Across the zephyr's heliotrope career;
I sit contentedly upon the moon
And watch the sunlight trickle round the sphere.

The shiny trill of jagged, feathered rocks
I hear with glee as swift I fly away;
And over waves of subtle, woolly flocks
Crashes the breaking day!

Anonymous.

[25]

THE MOON IS UP

THE moon is up, the moon is up!
  The larks begin to fly,
  And, like a drowsy buttercup,
Dark Phœbus skims the sky,
The elephant, with cheerful voice,
  Sings blithely on the spray;
The bats and beetles all rejoice,
  Then let me, too, be gay.

I would I were a porcupine,
  And wore a peacock's tail;
To-morrow, if the moon but shine,
  Perchance I'll be a whale.
Then let me, like the cauliflower,
  Be merry while I may,
And, ere there comes a sunny hour
  To cloud my heart, be gay!

Anonymous.

'T IS MIDNIGHT

'T IS midnight, and the setting sun
    Is slowly rising in the west;
    The rapid rivers slowly run,
The frog is on his downy nest.
The pensive goat and sportive cow,
Hilarious, leap from bough to bough.

Anonymous.

UPRISING SEE THE FITFUL LARK

UPRISING see the fitful lark
　　Unfold his pinion to the stream;
　　The pensive watch-dog's mellow bark
O'ershades yon cottage like a dream:
The playful duck and warbling bee
Hop gayly on, from tree to tree!

How calmly could my spirit rest
　　Beneath yon primrose bell so blue,
And watch those airy oxen drest
　　In every tint of pearling hue!
As on they hurl the gladsome plough,
While fairy zephyrs deck each brow!

Anonymous.

LIKE TO THE THUNDERING TONE

LIKE to the thundering tone of unspoke
　　　　speeches,
　　Or like a lobster clad in logic breeches,
Or like the gray fur of a crimson cat,
Or like the mooncalf in a slipshod hat;
E'en such is he who never was begotten
Until his children were both dead and rotten.

Like to the fiery tombstone of a cabbage,
Or like a crab-louse with its bag and baggage,
Or like the four square circle of a ring,
Or like to hey ding, ding-a, ding-a, ding;
E'en such is he who spake, and yet, no doubt,
Spake to small purpose, when his tongue was out.

Like to a fair, fresh, fading, wither'd rose,
Or like to rhyming verse that runs in prose,
Or like the stumbles of a tinder-box,
Or like a man that 's sound yet sickness mocks;
E'en such is he who died and yet did laugh
To see these lines writ for his epitaph.

Bishop Corbet
in 17th century.

MY DREAM

I DREAMED a dream next Tuesday week,
    Beneath the apple-trees;
    I thought my eyes were big pork-pies,
And my nose was Stilton cheese.
The clock struck twenty minutes to six,
    When a frog sat on my knee;
I asked him to lend me eighteenpence,
    But he borrowed a shilling of me.

Anonymous.

MY HOME

MY home is on the rolling deep,
   I spend my time a-feeding sheep;
   And when the waves on high are running,
I take my gun and go a-gunning.
I shoot wild ducks down deep snake-holes,
And drink gin-sling from two-quart bowls.

Anonymous.

IN IMMEMORIAM

WE seek to know, and knowing seek;
   We seek, we know, and every sense
   Is trembling with the great intense,
And vibrating to what we speak.

We ask too much, we seek too oft;
   We know enough and should no more;
   And yet we skim through Fancy's lore,
And look to earth and not aloft.

.   .   .   .

O Sea! whose ancient ripples lie
   On red-ribbed sands where seaweeds shone;
   O moon! whose golden sickle's gone,
O voices all! like you I die!

Cuthbert Bede.

THE HIGHER PANTHEISM IN A NUTSHELL

ONE, who is not, we see; but one, whom we
see not, is;
Surely, this is not that; but that is assuredly this.

What, and wherefore, and whence: for under is
over and under;
If thunder could be without lightning, lightning
could be without thunder.

Doubt is faith in the main; but faith, on the
whole, is doubt;
We cannot believe by proof; but could we believe
without?

Why, and whither, and how? for barley and rye
are not clover;
Neither are straight lines curves; yet over is under
and over.

One and two are not one; but one and nothing is
two;
Truth can hardly be false, if falsehood cannot be
true.

Parallels all things are; yet many of these are
    askew;
You are certainly I; but certainly I am not you.

One, whom we see not, is; and one, who is not,
    we see;
Fiddle, we know, is diddle; and diddle, we take it,
    is dee.

A. C. Swinburne.

DARWINITY

POWER to thine elbow, thou newest of
    sciences,
    All the old landmarks are ripe for decay;
Wars are but shadows, and so are alliances,
    Darwin the great is the man of the day.

All other 'ologies want an apology;
    Bread 's a mistake — Science offers a stone;
Nothing is true but Anthropobiology —
    Darwin the great understands it alone.

Mighty the great evolutionist teacher is,
    Licking Morphology clean into shape;
Lord! what an ape the Professor or Preacher is,
    Ever to doubt his descent from an ape.

Man 's an Anthropoid — he cannot help that, you
    know —
First evoluted from Pongos of old;
He 's but a branch of the *catarrhine* cat, you
    know —
Monkey I mean — that 's an ape with a cold.

Fast dying out are man's later Appearances,
    Cataclysmitic Geologies gone;
Now of Creation completed the clearance is,
    Darwin alone you must anchor upon.

Primitive Life — Organisms were chemical,
    Busting spontaneous under the sea;
Purely subaqueous, panaquademical,
    Was the original Crystal of Me.

I 'm the Apostle of mighty Darwinity,
    Stands for Divinity — sounds much the same —
Apo-theistico-Pan-Asininity
    Only can doubt whence the lot of us came.

Down on your knees, Superstition and Flunkey-
    dom!
Won't you accept such plain doctrines instead?
What is so simple as primitive Monkeydom
    Born in the sea with a cold in its head?

                   Herman Merivale.

SONG OF THE SCREW

A MOVING form or rigid mass,
    Under whate'er conditions
    Along successive screws must pass
    Between each two positions.
It turns around and slides along —
This is the burden of my song.

The pitch of screw, if multiplied
    By angle of rotation,
Will give the distance it must glide
    In motion of translation.
Infinite pitch means pure translation,
And zero pitch means pure rotation.

Two motions on two given screws,
    With amplitudes at pleasure,
Into a third screw-motion fuse;
    Whose amplitude we measure
By parallelogram construction
(A very obvious deduction.)

Its axis cuts the nodal line
    Which to both screws is normal,
And generates a form divine,
    Whose name, in language formal,
Is "surface-ruled of third degree."
Cylindroid is the name for me.

Rotation round a given line
    Is like a force along.
If to say couple you incline,
    You 're clearly in the wrong ; —
'T is obvious, upon reflection,
A line is not a mere direction.

So couples with translations too
    In all respects agree ;
And thus there centres in the screw
    A wondrous harmony
Of Kinematics and of Statics, —
The sweetest thing in mathematics.

The forces on one given screw,
    With motion on a second,
In general some work will do,
    Whose magnitude is reckoned
By angle, force, and what we call
The coefficient virtual.

Rotation now to force convert,
    And force into rotation ;
Unchanged the work, we can assert,
    In spite of transformation.
And if two screws no work can claim,
Reciprocal will be their name.

Five numbers will a screw define,
    A screwing motion, six ;
For four will give the axial line,
    One more the pitch will fix ;

And hence we always can contrive
One screw reciprocal to five.

Screws — two, three, four or five, combined
    (No question here of six),
Yield other screws which are confined
    Within one screw complex.
Thus we obtain the clearest notion
Of freedom and constraint of motion.

In complex III., three several screws
    At every point you find,
Or if you one direction choose,
    One screw is to your mind;
And complexes of order III.
Their own reciprocals may be.

In IV., wherever you arrive,
    You find of screws a cone,
On every line in complex V.
    There is precisely one;
At each point of this complex rich,
A plane of screws have given pitch.

But time would fail me to discourse
    Of Order and Degree;
Of Impulse, Energy and Force,
    And Reciprocity.
All these and more, for motions small,
Have been discussed by Dr. Ball.

Anonymous.

MOORLANDS OF THE NOT

ACROSS the moorlands of the Not
    We chase the gruesome When;
    And hunt the Itness of the What
Through forests of the Then.
Into the Inner Consciousness
    We track the crafty Where;
We spear the Ego tough, and beard
    The Selfhood in his lair.

With lassos of the brain we catch
    The Isness of the Was;
And in the copses of the Whence
    We hear the think bees buzz.
We climb the slippery Whichbark tree
    To watch the Thusness roll;
And pause betimes in gnostic rimes
    To woo the Over Soul.

Anonymous.

METAPHYSICS *

WHY and Wherefore set out one day
    To hunt for a wild Negation.
    They agreed to meet at a cool retreat
On the Point of Interrogation.

* By permission of the author; from " The Bashful Earthquake,"
copyright, 1898.

But the night was dark and they missed their mark,
   And, driven well-nigh to distraction,
They lost their ways in a murky maze
   Of utter abstruse abstraction.

Then they took a boat and were soon afloat
   On a sea of Speculation,
But the sea grew rough, and their boat, though tough,
   Was split into an Equation.

As they floundered about in the waves of doubt
   Rose a fearful Hypothesis,
Who gibbered with glee as they sank in the sea,
   And the last they saw was this :

On a rock-bound reef of Unbelief
   There sat the wild Negation ;
Then they sank once more and were washed ashore
   At the Point of Interrogation.

Oliver Herford.

ABSTROSOPHY *

IF echoes from the fitful past
   Could rise to mental view,
   Would all their fancied radiance last
Or would some odors from the blast,
   Untouched by Time, accrue ?

* By permission of the author; from " The Burgess Nonsense
Book," copyright, 1901.

Is present pain a future bliss,
  Or is it something worse ?
For instance, take a case like this :
Is fancied kick a real kiss,
  Or rather the reverse ?

Is plenitude of passion palled
  By poverty of scorn ?
Does Fiction mend where Fact has mauled ?
Has Death its wisest victims called
  When idiots are born ?

Gelett Burgess.

ABSTEMIA *

In Mystic Argot *often Confounded with Farrago*

IF aught that stumbles in my speech
    Or stutters in my pen,
  Or, claiming tribute, each to each,
  Rise, not to fall again,
Let something lowlier far, for me,
    Through evanescent shades —
Than which my spirit might not be
  Nourished in fitful ecstasy
Not less to know but more to see
  Where that great Bliss pervades.

Gelett Burgess.

* By permission of the author; from " The Burgess Nonsense
Book," copyright, 1901.

PSYCHOLOPHON *

Supposed to be Translated from the Old Parsee

TWINE then the rays
  Round her soft Theban tissues!
 All will be as She says,
When that dead past reissues.
Matters not what nor where,
 Hark, to the moon's dim cluster!
How was her heavy hair
 Lithe as a feather duster!
Matters not when nor whence;
 Flittertigibbet!
Sounds make the song, not sense,
 Thus I inhibit!

Gelett Burgess.

TIMON OF ARCHIMEDES †

AS one who cleaves the circumambient air
  Seeking in azure what it lacks in space,
 And sees a young and finely chiselled face
Filled with foretastes of wisdom yet more rare;
Touching and yet untouched — unmeasured grace!
 A breathing credo and a living prayer —
 Yet of the earth, still earthy; debonair
The while in heaven it seeketh for a place.

* By permission of the author; from "The Burgess Nonsense Book," copyright, 1901.

 † By permission of R. H. Russell; from "Just Rhymes," copyright, 1899.

So thy dear eyes and thy kind lips but say —
   Ere from his cerements Timon seems to flit :
     " What of the reaper grim with sickle keen ? "
And then the sunlight ushers in new day
   And for our tasks our bodies seem more fit —
     " Might of the night, unfleeing, sight unseen."

Charles Battell Loomis.

ALONE

ALONE ! Alone !
    I sit in the solitudes of the moonshades,
    Soul-hungering in the moonshade solitudes
      sit I —
My heart-lifts beaten down in the wild wind-path.
Oppressed, and scourged and beaten down are my
      heart-lifts.
I fix my gaze on the eye-star, and the eye-star flings
      its dart upon me.
I wonder why my soul is lost in wonder why I am,
And why the eye-star mocks me,
Why the wild wind beats down my heart-lifts ;
Why I am stricken here in the moonshade solitudes.
Oh ! why am I what I am,
And why am I anything ?
Am I not as wild as the wind and more crazy ?
Why do I sit in the moonshade, while the eye-
      star mocks me while I ask what I am ?
Why ? Why ?

Anonymous.

LINES BY A MEDIUM

I MIGHT not, if I could;
    I should not, if I might;
    Yet if I should I would,
And, shoulding, I should quite!

I must not, yet I may;
    I can, and still I must;
But ah! I cannot — nay,
    To must I may not, just!

I shall, although I will,
    But be it understood,
If I may, can, shall — still
    I might, could, would, or should!

Anonymous.

TRANSCENDENTALISM

IT is told, in Buddhi-theosophic schools,
        There are rules,
    By observing which, when mundane labor irks
One can simulate quiescence
By a timely evanescence
From his Active Mortal Essence,
    (Or his Works.)

[41]

The particular procedure leaves research
        In the lurch,
But, apparently, this matter-moulded form
        Is a kind of outer plaster,
        Which a well-instructed Master
        Can remove without disaster
            When he 's warm.

And to such as mourn an Indian Solar Clime
        At its prime
'T were a thesis most immeasurably fit,
        So expansively elastic,
        And so plausibly fantastic,
        That one gets enthusiastic
            For a bit.

From the Times of India.

INDIFFERENCE

IN loopy links the canker crawls,
        Tads twiddle in their 'polian glee,
        Yet sinks my heart as water falls.
The loon that laughs, the babe that bawls,
The wedding wear, the funeral palls,
        Are neither here nor there to me.
        Of life the mingled wine and brine
    I sit and sip pipslipsily.

Anonymous.

[42]

QUATRAIN

OH! to be wafted away
    From this black Aceldama of sorrow,
    Where the dust of an earthy to-day
Makes the earth of a dusty to-morrow.

Anonymous.

COSSIMBAZAR

COME fleetly, come fleetly, my hookabadar,
    For the sound of the tam-tam is heard from
      afar.
"Banoolah! Banoolah!" The Brahmins are nigh,
And the depths of the jungle re-echo their cry.
    Pestonjee Bomanjee!
    Smite the guitar;
Join in the chorus, my hookabadar.

Heed not the blast of the deadly monsoon,
Nor the blue Brahmaputra that gleams in the moon.
Stick to thy music, and oh, let the sound
Be heard with distinctness a mile or two round.
    Jamsetjee, Jeejeebhoy!
    Sweep the guitar.
Join in the chorus, my hookabadar.

[43]

Art thou a Buddhist, or dost thou indeed
Put faith in the monstrous Mohammedan creed?
Art thou a Ghebir — a blinded Parsee?
Not that it matters an atom to me.
   Cursetjee Bomanjee!
  Twang the guitar
Join in the chorus, my hookabadar.

      Henry S. Leigh.

THE PERSONIFIED
SENTIMENTAL*

AFFECTION'S charm no longer gilds
  The idol of the shrine;
  But cold Oblivion seeks to fill
Regret's ambrosial wine.
Though Friendship's offering buried lies
 'Neath cold Aversion's snow,
Regard and Faith will ever bloom
 Perpetually below.

I see thee whirl in marble halls,
 In Pleasure's giddy train;
Remorse is never on that brow,
 Nor Sorrow's mark of pain.
Deceit has marked thee for her own;
 Inconstancy the same;
And Ruin wildly sheds its gleam
 Athwart thy path of shame.

      Bret Harte.

* By permission of Houghton, Mifflin & Co., authorized publishers
of Bret Harte's works.

A CLASSIC ODE *

OH, limpid stream of Tyrus, now I hear
 The pulsing wings of Armageddon's host,
 Clear as a colcothar and yet more clear —
(Twin orbs, like those of which the Parsees
 boast;)

Down in thy pebbled deeps in early spring
 The dimpled naiads sport, as in the time
When Ocidelus with untiring wing
 Drave teams of prancing tigers, 'mid the chime

Of all the bells of Phicol. Scarcely one
 Peristome veils its beauties now, but then —
Like nascent diamonds, sparkling in the sun,
 Or sainfoin, circinate, or moss in marshy fen.

Loud as the blasts of Tubal, loud and strong,
 Sweet as the songs of Sappho, aye more sweet;
Long as the spear of Arnon, twice as long,
 What time he hurled it at King Pharaoh's feet.

     Charles Battell Loomis.

WHERE AVALANCHES WAIL

WHERE avalanches wail, and green Distress
 Sweeps o'er the pallid beak of loveliness:
 Where melancholy Sulphur holds her sway:
And cliffs of conscience tremble and obey;

 * By permission of R. H. Russell; from "Just Rhymes," copyright, 1899.

[45]

And where Tartarean rattlesnakes expire;
Twisting like tendrils of a hero's pyre?
No! dancing in the meteor's hall of power,
See, Genius ponders o'er Affection's tower!
A form of thund'ring import soars on high,
Hark! 't is the gore of infant melody:
No more shall verdant Innocence amuse
The lips that death-fraught Indignation glues; —
Tempests shall teach the trackless tide of thought,
That undiminish'd senselessness is naught;
Freedom shall glare; and oh! ye links divine,
The Poet's heart shall quiver in the brine.

Anonymous.

BLUE MOONSHINE

M INGLED aye with fragrant yearnings,
　　Throbbing in the mellow glow,
　　Glint the silvery spirit-burnings,
Pearly blandishments of woe.

Aye! forever and forever,
　Whilst the love-lorn censers sweep,
Whilst the jasper winds dissever
　Amber-like the crystal deep,

Shall the soul's delirious slumber,
　Sea-green vengeance of a kiss,
Teach despairing crags to number
　Blue infinities of bliss.

Francis G. Stokes.

NONSENSE

GOOD reader, if you e'er have seen,
    When Phœbus hastens to his pillow,
  The mermaids with their tresses green
Dancing upon the western billow;
    If you have seen at twilight dim,
    When the lone spirit's vesper hymn
Floats wild along the winding shore,
  The fairy train their ringlets weave
    Glancing along the spangled green; —
    If you have seen all this, and more,
  God bless me! what a deal you 've seen!

Thomas Moore.

SUPERIOR NONSENSE VERSES

HE comes with herald clouds of dust;
    Ecstatic frenzies rend his breast;
  A moment, and he graced the earth —
Now, seek him at the eagle's nest.

Hark! see'st thou not the torrent's flash
  Far shooting o'er the mountain height?
Hear'st not the billow's solemn roar,
  That echoes through the vaults of night?

Anon the murky cloud is riven,
  The lightnings leap in sportive play,
And through the clanging doors of heaven,
  In calm effulgence bursts the day.

Hope, peering from her fleecy car,
    Smiles welcome to the coming spring,
And birds with blithesome songs of praise
    Make every grove and valley ring.

What though on pinions of the blast
    The sea-gulls sweep with leaden flight ?
What though the watery caverns deep
    Gleam ghostly on the wandering sight ?

Is there no music in the trees
    To charm thee with its frolic mirth ?
Must Care's wan phantom still beguile
    And chain thee to the stubborn earth ?

Lo ! Fancy from her magic realm
    Pours Boreal gleams adown the pole.
The tidal currents lift and swell —
    Dead currents of the ocean's soul.

Yet never may their mystic streams
    Breathe whispers of the mournful past,
Or Pallas wake her sounding lyre
    Mid Ether's columned temples vast.

Grave History walks again the earth
    As erst it did in days of eld,
When seated on the golden throne
    Her hand a jewelled sceptre held.

The Delphian oracle is dumb,
    Dread Cumae wafts no words of fate,
To fright the eager souls that press
    Through sullen Lethe's iron gate.

But deeper shadows gather o'er
   The vales that sever night and morn;
And darkness folds with brooding wing
   The rustling fields of waving corn.

Then issuing from his bosky lair
   The crafty tiger crouches low,
Or thunders from the frozen north
   The white bear lapped in Arctic snow.

Thus shift the scenes till high aloft
   The young moon sets her crescent horn,
And in gray evening's emerald sea
   The beauteous Star of Love is born.

Anonymous.

WHEN MOONLIKE ORE THE HAZURE SEAS

WHEN moonlike ore the hazure seas
   In soft effulgence swells,
     When silver jews and balmy breaze
Bend down the Lily's bells ;
When calm and deap, the rosy sleap
   Has lapt your soal in dreems,
R Hangeline ! R lady mine !
   Dost thou remember Jeames ?

I mark thee in the Marble all,
   Where England's loveliest shine —
I say the fairest of them hall
   Is Lady Hangeline.

[49]

My soul, in desolate eclipse,
　　With recollection teems —
And then I hask, with weeping lips,
　　Dost thou remember Jeames?

Away! I may not tell thee hall
　　This soughring heart endures —
There is a lonely sperrit-call
　　That Sorrow never cures;
There is a little, little Star,
　　That still above me beams;
It is the Star of Hope — but ar!
　　Dost thou remember Jeames?

W. M. Thackeray.

LINES BY A PERSON OF QUALITY

FLUTTERING spread thy purple pinions,
　　Gentle Cupid, o'er my heart,
　　I a slave in thy dominions,
Nature must give way to art.

Mild Arcadians, ever blooming,
　　Nightly nodding o'er your flocks,
See my weary days consuming,
　　All beneath yon flowery rocks.

Thus the Cyprian goddess weeping,
　　Mourned Adonis, darling youth:
Him the boar, in silence creeping,
　　Gored with unrelenting tooth.

Cynthia, tune harmonious numbers ;
    Fair Discretion, tune the lyre ;
Soothe my ever-waking slumbers ;
    Bright Apollo, lend thy choir.

Gloomy Pluto, king of terrors,
    Armed in adamantine chains,
Lead me to the crystal mirrors,
    Watering soft Elysian plains.

Mournful Cypress, verdant willow,
    Gilding my Aurelia's brows,
Morpheus, hovering o'er my pillow,
    Hear me pay my dying vows.

Melancholy, smooth Mæander,
    Swiftly purling in a round,
On thy margin lovers wander
    With thy flowery chaplets crowned.

Thus when Philomela, drooping,
    Softly seeks her silent mate,
So the bird of Juno stooping ;
    Melody resigns to fate.

Alexander Pope.

FRANGIPANNI

UNTWINE those ringlets ! Ev'ry dainty clasp
    That shines like twisted sunlight in my eye
  Is but the coiling of the jewelled asp
That smiles to see men die.

[51]

Oh, cobra-curlèd! Fierce-fanged fair one! Draw
   Night's curtain o'er the landscape of thy hair!
I yield! I kneel! I own, I bless thy law
   That dooms me to despair.

I mark the crimson ruby of thy lips,
   I feel the witching weirdness of thy breath!
I droop! I sink into my soul's eclipse, —
   I fall in love with death!

And yet, vouchsafe a moment! I would gaze
   Once more into those sweetly-murderous eyes,
Soft glimmering athwart the pearly haze
   That smites to dusk the skies.

Hast thou no pity? Must I darkly tread
   The unknown paths that lead me wide from
     thee?
Hast thou no garland for this aching head
   That soon so low must be?

No sound? No sigh? No smile? Is *all* forgot?
   Then spin my shroud out of that golden skein
Thou callst thy tresses! *I* shall stay thee not —
   My struggles were but vain!

But shall I see thee far beyond the sun,
   When the new dawn lights Empyrean scenes?
What matters now? I know the poem 's done,
   And wonder what the dickens it all means!

Anonymous.

LINES BY A FOND LOVER

LOVELY maid, with rapture swelling,
    Should these pages meet thine eye,
    Clouds of absence soft dispelling; —
Vacant memory heaves a sigh.

As the rose, with fragrance weeping,
    Trembles to the tuneful wave,
So my heart shall twine unsleeping,
    Till it canopies the grave.

Though another's smile 's requited,
    Envious fate my doom should be;
Joy forever disunited,
    Think, ah! think, at times on me!

Oft, amid the spicy gloaming,
    Where the brakes their songs instil,
Fond affection silent roaming,
    Loves to linger by the rill —

There, when echo's voice consoling,
    Hears the nightingale complain,
Gentle sighs my lips controlling,
    Bind my soul in beauty's chain.

Oft in slumber's deep recesses,
    I thy mirror'd image see;
Fancy mocks the vain caresses
    I would lavish like a bee!

[53]

But how vain is glittering sadness!
　Hark, I hear distraction's knell!
Torture gilds my heart with madness!
　Now forever fare thee well!

Anonymous.

FORCING A WAY

HOW many strive to force a way
　　Where none can go save those who pay,
　　To verdant plains of soft delight
The homage of the silent night,
When countless stars from pole to pole
Around the earth unceasing roll
In roseate shadow's silvery hue,
Shine forth and gild the morning dew.

And must we really part for good,
But meet again here where we 've stood?
No more delightful trysting-place,
We 've watched sweet Nature's smiling face.
No more the landscape's lovely brow,
Exchange our mutual breathing vow.
Then should the twilight draw around
No loving interchange of sound.

Less for renown than innate love,
These to my wish must recreant prove;
Nor whilst an impulse here remain,
Can ever hope the soul to gain;

[54]

For memory scanning all the past,
Relaxes her firm bonds at last,
And gives to candor all the grace
The heart can in its temple trace.

Anonymous.

THY HEART

THY heart is like some icy lake,
   On whose cold brink I stand;
   Oh, buckle on my spirit's skate,
And lead, thou living saint, the way
   To where the ice is thin —
That it may break beneath my feet
   And let a lover in!

Anonymous.

A LOVE-SONG BY A LUNATIC

THERE's not a spider in the sky,
   There's not a glowworm in the sea,
   There's not a crab that soars on high,
But bids me dream, dear maid, of thee!

When watery Phœbus ploughs the main,
   When fiery Luna gilds the lea,
As flies run up the window-pane,
   So fly my thoughts, dear love, to thee!

Anonymous.

THE PARTERRE

I DON'T know any greatest treat
   As sit him in a gay parterre,
     And sniff one up the perfume sweet
Of every roses buttoning there.

It only want my charming miss
   Who make to blush the self red rose;
Oh! I have envy of to kiss
   The end's tip of her splendid nose.

Oh! I have envy of to be
   What grass 'neath her pantoffle push,
And too much happy seemeth me
   The margaret which her vestige crush.

But I will meet her nose at nose,
   And take occasion for her hairs,
And indicate her all my woes,
   That she in fine agree my prayers.

THE ENVOY

I don't know any greatest treat
   As sit him in a gay parterre,
With Madame who is too more sweet
   Than every roses buttoning there.

                  E. H. Palmer.

TO MOLLIDUSTA

WHEN gooseberries grow on the stem of a
　　daisy,
　　And plum-puddings roll on the tide to
　　　　the shore,
And julep is made from the curls of a jazey,
　　Oh, then, Mollidusta, I 'll love thee no more.

When steamboats no more on the Thames shall
　　be going,
　　And a cast-iron bridge reach Vauxhall from the
　　　　Nore,
And the Grand Junction waterworks cease to be
　　flowing,
　　Oh, then, Mollidusta, I 'll love thee no more.

Planché.

JOHN JONES

At the Piano

I

LOVE me and leave me; what love bids re-
　　trieve me? can June's fist grasp May?
　　Leave me and love me; hopes eyed once
　　　　above me like spring's sprouts, decay;
Fall as the snow falls, when summer leaves grow
　　false — cards packed for storm's play!

II

Nay, say Decay's self be but last May's elf, wing
    shifted, eye sheathed —
Changeling in April's crib rocked, who lets 'scape
    rills locked fast since frost breathed —
Skin cast (think!) adder-like, now bloom bursts
    bladder-like, — bloom frost bequeathed?

III

Ah, how can fear sit and hear as love hears it
    grief's heart's cracked grate's screech?
Chance lets the gate sway that opens on hate's way
    and shews on shame's beach
Crouched like an imp sly change watch sweet love's
    shrimps lie, a toothful in each.

IV

Time feels his tooth slip on husks wet from Truth's
    lip, which drops them and grins —
Shells where no throb stirs of life left in lobsters
    since joy thrilled their fins —
Hues of the pawn's tail or comb that makes dawn
    stale, so red for our sins!

V

Leaves love last year smelt now feel dead love's
    tears melt — flies caught in time's mesh!
Salt are the dews in which new time breeds new
    sin, brews blood and stews flesh;
Next year may see dead more germs than this
    weeded and reared them afresh.

VI

Old times left perish, new time to cherish; life
    just shifts its tune;
As, when the day dies, half afraid, eyes the growth
    of the moon;
Love me and save me, take me or waive me;
    death takes one so soon!

A. C. Swinburne.

THE OWL AND THE PUSSY–CAT

THE Owl and the Pussy-Cat went to sea
    In a beautiful pea-green boat: ·
    They took some honey, and plenty of money
Wrapped up in a five-pound note.
The Owl looked up to the stars above,
    And sang to a small guitar,
"Oh, lovely Pussy, oh, Pussy, my love,
    What a beautiful Pussy you are,
        You are,
        You are!
What a beautiful Pussy you are!"

Pussy said to the Owl, "You elegant fowl,
    How charmingly sweet you sing!
Oh, let us be married; too long we have tarried:
    But what shall we do for a ring?"

They sailed away for a year and a day,
  To the land where the bong-tree grows;
And there in the wood a Piggy-wig stood,
  With a ring at the end of his nose,
      His nose,
      His nose,
  With a ring at the end of his nose.

"Dear Pig, are you willing to sell for one shilling
  Your ring?" Said the Piggy, "I will."
So they took it away and were married next day
  By the Turkey who lives on the hill.
They dined on mince and slices of quince,
  Which they ate with a runcible spoon;
And hand in hand, on the edge of the sand,
  They danced by the light of the moon,
      The moon,
      The moon,
  They danced by the light of the moon.

Edward Lear.

A BALLADE OF THE NURSERIE

SHE hid herself in the *soirée* kettle
    Out of her Ma's way, wise, wee maid!
    Wan was her lip as the lily's petal,
Sad was the smile that over it played.

Why doth she warble not? Is she afraid
Of the hound that howls, or the moaning mole?
   Can it be on an errand she hath delayed?
Hush thee, hush thee, dear little soul!

The nightingale sings to the nodding nettle
   In the gloom o' the gloaming athwart the glade:
The zephyr sighs soft on Popòcatapètl,
   And Auster is taking it cool in the shade:
   Sing, hey, for a *gutta serenade!*
Not mine to stir up a storied pole,
   No noses snip with a bluggy blade —
Hush thee, hush thee, dear little soul!

Shall I bribe with a store of minted metal?
   With Everton toffee thee persuade?
That thou in a kettle thyself shouldst settle,
   When grandly and gaudily all arrayed!
   Thy flounces 'ill foul and fangles fade.
Come out, and Algernon Charles 'ill roll
   Thee safe and snug in Plutonian plaid —
Hush thee, hush thee, dear little soul!

Envoi

When nap is none and raiment frayed,
And winter crowns the puddered poll,
   A kettle sings ane soote ballade —
Hush thee, hush thee, dear little soul.

John Twig.

A BALLAD OF HIGH ENDEAVOR

AH Night ! blind germ of days to be,
    Ah me ! ah me !
    (Sweet Venus, mother !)
What wail of smitten strings hear we ?
    (Ah me ! ah me !
        Hey diddle dee !)

Ravished by clouds our Lady Moon,
    Ah me ! ah me !
    (Sweet Venus, mother !)
Sinks swooning in a lady-swoon
    (Ah me ! ah me !
        Dum diddle dee !)

What profits it to rise i' the dark ?
    Ah me ! ah me !
    (Sweet Venus, mother !)
If love but over-soar its mark
    (Ah me ! ah me !
        Hey diddle dee !)

What boots to fall again forlorn ?
    Ah me ! ah me !
    (Sweet Venus, mother !)
Scorned by the grinning hound of scorn,
    (Ah me ! ah me !
        Dum diddle dee !)

Art thou not greater who art less?
　　Ah me! ah me!
　　(Sweet Venus, mother!)
Low love fulfilled of low success?
　　(Ah me! ah me!
　　　　Hey diddle dee!)
　　　　　　　　Anonymous.

THE LUGUBRIOUS WHING-WHANG *

OUT on the margin of moonshine land,
　　Tickle me, love, in these lonesome ribs,
　　Out where the whing-whang loves to stand,
Writing his name with his tail on the sand,
And wiping it out with his oogerish hand;
　　Tickle me, love, in these lonesome ribs.

Is it the gibber of gungs and keeks?
　　Tickle me, love, in these lonesome ribs,
Or what *is* the sound the whing-whang seeks,
Crouching low by the winding creeks,
And holding his breath for weeks and weeks?
　　Tickle me, love, in these lonesome ribs.

Aroint him the wraithest of wraithly things!
　　Tickle me, love, in these lonesome ribs,
'T is a fair whing-whangess with phosphor rings,
And bridal jewels of fangs and stings,

* By permission of the author; from "Rhymes of Childhood," copyright, 1890, 1898.

[63]

And she sits and as sadly and softly sings
As the mildewed whir of her own dead wings;
Tickle me, dear; tickle me here;
Tickle me, love, in these lonesome ribs.

James Whitcomb Riley.

OH! WEARY MOTHER

THE lilies lie in my lady's bower,
    (Oh! weary mother, drive the cows to
        roost;)
They faintly droop for a little hour;
My lady's head droops like a flower.

She took the porcelain in her hand,
    (Oh! weary mother, drive the cows to roost;)
She poured; I drank at her command;
Drank deep, and now — you understand!
    (Oh! weary mother, drive the cows to roost.)

Barry Pain.

SWISS AIR *

I'M a gay tra, la, la,
    With my fal, lal, la, la,
    And my bright —
And my light —
    Tra, la, le.   [*Repeat.*]

* By permission of Houghton, Mifflin & Co., authorized publishers
of Bret Harte's works.

Then laugh, ha, ha, ha,
And ring, ting, ling, ling,
And sing, fal, la, la,
    La, la, le.   *[Repeat.]*

                  Bret Harte.

THE BULBUL*

THE bulbul hummeth like a book
    Upon the pooh-pooh tree,
And now and then he takes a look
    At you and me,
    At me and you.
    Kuchi!
    Kuchoo!

                  Owen Seaman.

BALLAD

With an Ancient Refrain

O STOODENT A has gone and spent,
    With a hey-lililu and a how-low-lan
    All his money to a Cent,
And the birk and the broom blooms bonny.

His Creditors he could not pay,
With a hey-lililu and a how-low-lan,
And Prison proved a shock to A,
And the birk and the broom blooms bonny.

                  Anonymous.

* By permission of John Lane; from "The Battle of the Bays."

OH, MY GERALDINE

OH, my Geraldine,
    No flow'r was ever seen so toodle um.
    You are my lum ti toodle lay,
      Pretty, pretty queen,
Is rum ti Geraldine and something teen,
More sweet than tiddle lum in May.
     Like the star so bright
     That somethings all the night,
      My Geraldine!
You're fair as the rum ti lum ti sheen,
    Hark! there is what — ho!
    From something — um, you know,
     Dear, what I mean.
Oh! rum! tum!! tum!!! my Geraldine.

               F. C. Burnand.

BUZ, QUOTH THE BLUE FLY

BUZ, quoth the blue fly,
    Hum, quoth the bee,
    Buz and hum they cry,
     And so do we:
In his ear, in his nose, thus, do you see?
He ate the dormouse, else it was he.

            Ben Jonson
        in " The Masque of Oberon."

A SONG ON KING WILLIAM III

AS I walked by myself,
       And talked to myself,
              Myself said unto me,
Look to thyself,
Take care of thyself,
       For nobody cares for thee.

I answered myself,
And said to myself,
       In the self-same repartee,
Look to thyself,
Or not look to thyself,
       The selfsame thing will be.

Anonymous.

THERE WAS A MONKEY

THERE was a monkey climbed up a tree,
       When he fell down, then down fell he.

There was a crow sat on a stone,
When he was gone, then there was none.

There was an old wife did eat an apple,
When she had eat two, she had eat a couple.

There was a horse going to the mill,
When he went on, he stood not still.

There was a butcher cut his thumb,
When it did bleed, then blood did come.

There was a lackey ran a race,
When he ran fast, he ran apace.

There was a cobbler clouting shoon,
When they were mended, they were done.

There was a chandler making candle,
When he them strip, he did them handle.

There was a navy went into Spain,
When it returned, it came again.

Anonymous, 1626.

THE GUINEA PIG

THERE was a little Guinea-pig,
    Who, being little, was not big;
    He always walked upon his feet,
And never fasted when he eat.

When from a place he ran away,
He never at that place did stay;
And while he ran, as I am told,
He ne'er stood still for young or old.

He often squeaked, and sometimes vi'lent,
And when he squeaked he ne'er was silent :
Though ne'er instructed by a cat,
He knew a mouse was not a rat.

One day, as I am certified,
He took a whim, and fairly died ;
And as I'm told by men of sense,
He never has been living since !

Anonymous.

THREE CHILDREN

THREE children sliding on the ice
 Upon a summer's day,
  As it fell out they all fell in,
 The rest they ran away.

Now, had these children been at home,
 Or sliding on dry ground,
Ten thousand pounds to one penny
 They had not all been drowned.

You parents all that children have,
 And you too that have none,
If you would have them safe abroad
 Pray keep them safe at home.

London, 1662.

IF

IF all the land were apple-pie,
　　And all the sea were ink;
　　And all the trees were bread and cheese,
What should we do for drink?

Anonymous.

A RIDDLE

THE man in the wilderness asked of me
　　How many strawberries grew in the sea.
　　I answered him as I thought good,
As many as red herrings grow in the wood.

Anonymous.

THREE JOVIAL HUNTSMEN

THERE were three jovial huntsmen,
　　As I have heard them say,
　　And they would go a-hunting
All on a summer's day.

All the day they hunted,
　　And nothing could they find
But a ship a-sailing,
　　A-sailing with the wind.

One said it was a ship,
　The other said Nay ;
The third said it was a house
　With the chimney blown away.

And all the night they hunted,
　And nothing could they find ;
But the moon a-gliding,
　A-gliding with the wind.

One said it was the moon,
　The other said Nay ;
The third said it was a cheese,
　And half o't cut away.

　　　　　　　　　　　Anonymous.

THREE ACRES OF LAND

MY father left me three acres of land,
　　Sing ivy, sing ivy;
　My father left me three acres of land,
Sing holly, go whistle, and ivy!

I ploughed it with a ram's horn,
　Sing ivy, sing ivy ;
And sowed it all over with one peppercorn,
　Sing holly, go whistle, and ivy!

I harrowed it with a bramble bush,
    Sing ivy, sing ivy ;
And reaped it with my little penknife,
    Sing holly, go whistle, and ivy !

I got the mice to carry it to the barn,
    Sing ivy, sing ivy ;
And thrashed it with a goose's quill,
    Sing holly, go whistle, and ivy !

I got the cat to carry it to the mill,
    Sing ivy, sing ivy ;
The miller he swore he would have her paw,
And the cat she swore she would scratch his face,
    Sing holly, go whistle, and ivy !

Anonymous.

MASTER AND MAN

MASTER I have, and I am his man,
    Gallop a dreary dun ;
    Master I have, and I am his man,
And I 'll get a wife as fast as I can ;
With a heighly gaily gamberally,
    Higgledy piggledy, niggledy, niggledy,
    Gallop a dreary dun.

Anonymous.

HYDER IDDLE

HYDER iddle diddle dell,
    A yard of pudding is not an ell;
    Not forgetting tweedle-dye,
A tailor's goose will never fly.

Anonymous.

KING ARTHUR

WHEN good King Arthur ruled the land,
    He was a goodly king :
    He stole three pecks of barley meal,
To make a bag-pudding.

A bag-pudding the king did make,
    And stuffed it well with plums ;
And in it put great lumps of fat,
    As big as my two thumbs.

The king and queen did eat thereof,
    And noblemen beside ;
And what they could not eat that night,
    The queen next morning fried.

Anonymous.

[73]

IN THE DUMPS

WE 're all in the dumps,
    For diamonds are trumps;
      The kittens are gone to St. Paul's!
The babies are bit,
The moon 's in a fit,
And the houses are built without walls.

Anonymous.

TWEEDLE–DUM AND
TWEEDLE–DEE

TWEEDLE-DUM and Tweedle-dee
    Resolved to have a battle,
      For Tweedle-dum said Tweedle-dee
Had spoiled his nice new rattle.
Just then flew by a monstrous crow,
    As big as a tar-barrel,
Which frightened both the heroes so
    They quite forgot their quarrel.

Anonymous.

MARTIN TO HIS MAN

MARTIN said to his man,
    Fie! man, fie!
      Oh, Martin said to his man,
    Who's the fool now?
Martin said to his man,

Fill thou the cup, and I the can ;
Thou hast well drunken, man :
   Who 's the fool now ?

I see a sheep shearing corn,
   Fie ! man, fie !
I see a sheep shearing corn,
   Who 's the fool now ?
I see a sheep shearing corn,
And a cuckoo blow his horn ;
Thou hast well drunken, man :
   Who 's the fool now ?

I see a man in the moon,
   Fie ! man, fie !
I see a man in the moon,
   Who 's the fool now ?
I see a man in the moon,
Clouting of St. Peter's shoon,
Thou hast well drunken, man :
   Who 's the fool now ?

I see a hare chase a hound,
   Fie ! man, fie !
I see a hare chase a hound,
   Who 's the fool now ?
I see a hare chase a hound,
Twenty mile above the ground ;
Thou hast well drunken, man :
   Who 's the fool now ?

I see a goose ring a hog,
    Fie! man, fie!
I see a goose ring a hog,
    Who's the fool now?
I see a goose ring a hog,
And a snail that bit a dog;
Thou hast well drunken, man:
    Who's the fool now?

I see a mouse catch the cat,
    Fie! man, fie!
I see a mouse catch the cat,
    Who's the fool now?
I see a mouse catch the cat,
And the cheese to eat the rat;
Thou hast well drunken, man:
    Who's the fool now?

From *Deuteromelia*
printed in the reign of James I.

THE YONGHY-BONGHY-BO

I

ON the Coast of Coromandel
    Where the early pumpkins blow,
    In the middle of the woods
Lived the Yonghy-Bonghy-Bo.
Two old chairs, and half a candle,
One old jug without a handle, —

These were all his worldly goods :
In the middle of the woods,
These were all the worldly goods
Of the Yonghy-Bonghy-Bo,
Of the Yonghy-Bonghy-Bo.

II

Once, among the Bong-trees walking
Where the early pumpkins blow,
To a little heap of stones
Came the Yonghy-Bonghy-Bo.
There he heard a Lady talking,
To some milk-white Hens of Dorking, —
"'T is the Lady Jingly Jones !
On that little heap of stones
Sits the Lady Jingly Jones !"
Said the Yonghy-Bonghy-Bo,
Said the Yonghy-Bonghy-Bo.

III

"Lady Jingly ! Lady Jingly !
Sitting where the pumpkins blow,
Will you come and be my wife ?"
Said the Yonghy-Bonghy-Bo,
"I am tired of living singly, —
On this coast so wild and shingly, —
I'm a-weary of my life ;
If you'll come and be my wife,
Quite serene would be my life !"
Said the Yonghy-Bonghy-Bo,
Said the Yonghy-Bonghy-Bo.

IV

" On this Coast of Coromandel
    Shrimps and watercresses grow,
        Prawns are plentiful and cheap,"
    Said the Yonghy-Bonghy-Bo.
" You shall have my chairs and candle,
And my jug without a handle !
        Gaze upon the rolling deep
        (Fish is plentiful and cheap):
        As the sea, my love is deep ! "
    Said the Yonghy-Bonghy-Bo,
    Said the Yonghy-Bonghy-Bo.

V

Lady Jingly answered sadly,
    And her tears began to flow, —
        " Your proposal comes too late,
    Mr. Yonghy-Bonghy-Bo !
I would be your wife most gladly ! "
(Here she twirled her fingers madly,)
        " But in England I 've a mate !
        Yes ! you 've asked me far too late,
        For in England I 've a mate,
    Mr. Yonghy-Bonghy-Bo !
    Mr. Yonghy-Bonghy-Bo !

VI

" Mr. Jones (his name is Handel, —
    Handel Jones, Esquire & Co.)
        Dorking fowls delights to send,
    Mr. Yonghy-Bonghy-Bo !

Keep, oh, keep your chairs and candle,
And your jug without a handle, —
   I can merely be your friend !
   Should my Jones more Dorkings send,
   I will give you three, my friend !
Mr. Yonghy-Bonghy-Bo !
Mr. Yonghy-Bonghy-Bo !

VII

" Though you 've such a tiny body,
   And your head so large doth grow, —
   Though your hat may blow away,
Mr. Yonghy-Bonghy-Bo !
Though you 're such a Hoddy Doddy,
Yet I wish that I could modi-
   fy the words I needs must say !
   Will you please to go away ?
   That is all I have to say,
Mr. Yonghy-Bonghy-Bo !
Mr. Yonghy-Bonghy-Bo ! "

VIII

Down the slippery slopes of Myrtle,
   Where the early pumpkins blow,
   To the calm and silent sea
Fled the Yonghy-Bonghy-Bo.
There, beyond the Bay of Gurtle,
Lay a large and lively Turtle.
   " You 're the Cove,'' he said, " for me :
   On your back beyond the sea,
   Turtle, you shall carry me ! "

Said the Yonghy-Bonghy-Bo,
Said the Yonghy-Bonghy-Bo.

IX

Through the silent roaring ocean
  Did the Turtle swiftly go;
    Holding fast upon his shell
  Rode the Yonghy-Bonghy-Bo.
With a sad primæval motion
Toward the sunset isles of Boshen
    Still the Turtle bore him well,
    Holding fast upon his shell.
    "Lady Jingly Jones, farewell!"
  Sang the Yonghy-Bonghy-Bo,
  Sang the Yonghy-Bonghy-Bo.

X

From the Coast of Coromandel
  Did that Lady never go,
    On that heap of stones she mourns
  For the Yonghy-Bonghy-Bo.
On that Coast of Coromandel,
In his jug without a handle
    Still she weeps, and daily moans;
    On the little heap of stones
    To her Dorking Hens she moans,
  For the Yonghy-Bonghy-Bo,
  For the Yonghy-Bonghy-Bo.

Edward Lear.

THE POBBLE WHO HAS NO TOES

THE Pobble who has no toes
    Had once as many as we;
    When they said, " Some day you may lose
      them all,"
He replied, " Fish fiddle de-dee ! "
And his Aunt Jobiska made him drink
Lavender water tinged with pink ;
For she said, " The World in general knows
There 's nothing so good for a Pobble's toes ! "

The Pobble who has no toes
    Swam across the Bristol Channel ;
But before he set out he wrapped his nose
    In a piece of scarlet flannel.
For his Aunt Jobiska said, " No harm
Can come to his toes if his nose is warm ;
And it 's perfectly known that a Pobble's toes
Are safe — provided he minds his nose."

The Pobble swam fast and well,
    And when boats or ships came near him,
He tinkledy-binkledy-winkled a bell
    So that all the world could hear him.
And all the Sailors and Admirals cried,
When they saw him nearing the farther side,
" He has gone to fish for his Aunt Jobiska's
Runcible Cat with crimson whiskers ! "

But before he touched the shore —
 The shore of the Bristol Channel,
A sea-green Porpoise carried away
 His wrapper of scarlet flannel.
And when he came to observe his feet,
Formerly garnished with toes so neat,
His face at once became forlorn
On perceiving that all his toes were gone!

And nobody ever knew,
 From that dark day to the present,
Whoso had taken the Pobble's toes,
 In a manner so far from pleasant.
Whether the shrimps or crawfish gray,
Or crafty mermaids stole them away,
Nobody knew; and nobody knows
How the Pobble was robbed of his twice five toes!

The Pobble who has no toes
 Was placed in a friendly Bark,
And they rowed him back and carried him up
 To his Aunt Jobiska's Park.
And she made him a feast at his earnest wish,
Of eggs and buttercups fried with fish;
And she said, " It 's a fact the whole world knows,
That Pobbles are happier without their toes."

Edward Lear.

THE JUMBLIES

I

THEY went to sea in a sieve, they did;
   In a sieve they went to sea:
     In spite of all their friends could say,
On a winter's morn, on a stormy day,
   In a sieve they went to sea.
And when the sieve turned round and round,
And every one cried, " You 'll all be drowned ! "
They called aloud, " Our sieve ain't big ;
But we don't care a button, we don't care a fig :
   In a sieve we 'll go to sea ! "
     Far and few, far and few,
       Are the lands where the Jumblies live;
     Their heads are green and their hands are
       blue ;
     And they went to sea in a sieve.

II

They sailed away in a sieve, they did,
   In a sieve they sailed so fast,
With only a beautiful pea-green veil
Tied with a ribbon by way of a sail,
   To a small tobacco-pipe mast.
And every one said who saw them go,
" Oh ! won't they soon be upset, you know ?
For the sky is dark and the voyage is long,
And, happen what may, it 's extremely wrong
   In a sieve to sail so fast."

Far and few, far and few,
  Are the lands where the Jumblies live;
Their heads are green and their hands are
    blue;
And they went to sea in a sieve.

III

The water it soon came in, it did;
  The water it soon came in:
So, to keep them dry, they wrapped their feet
In a pinky paper all folded neat;
  And they fastened it down with a pin.
And they passed the night in a crockery-jar;
And each of them said, " How wise we are!
Though the sky be dark, and the voyage be long,
Yet we never can think we were rash or wrong,
  While round in our sieve we spin."
    Far and few, far and few,
      Are the lands where the Jumblies live;
    Their heads are green and their hands are
        blue;
    And they went to sea in a sieve.

IV

And all night long they sailed away;
  And when the sun went down,
They whistled and warbled a moony song
To the echoing sound of a coppery gong,
  In the shade of the mountains brown.
" O Timballoo! How happy we are
When we live in a sieve and a crockery-jar!

And all night long, in the moonlight pale,
We sail away with a pea-green sail
  In the shade of the mountains brown."
    Far and few, far and few,
      Are the lands where the Jumblies live;
    Their heads are green, and their hands are
        blue;
      And they went to sea in a sieve.

V

They sailed to the Western Sea, they did, —
  To a land all covered with trees;
And they bought an owl and a useful cart,
And a pound of rice, and a cranberry-tart,
  And a hive of silvery bees;
And they bought a pig, and some green jackdaws,
And a lovely monkey with lollipop paws,
And forty bottles of ring-bo-ree,
  And no end of Stilton cheese.
    Far and few, far and few,
      Are the lands where the Jumblies live;
    Their heads are green, and their hands are
        blue;
      And they went to sea in a sieve.

VI

And in twenty years they all came back, —
  In twenty years or more;
And every one said, " How tall they 've grown !
For they 've been to the Lakes, and the Torrible
    Zone,
  And the hills of the Chankly Bore."

And they drank their health, and gave them a feast
Of dumplings made of beautiful yeast;
And every one said, " If we only live,
We, too, will go to sea in a sieve,
    To the hills of the Chankly Bore."
        Far and few, far and few,
            Are the lands where the Jumblies live;
        Their heads are green, and their hands are
                blue;
            And they went to sea in a sieve.

Edward Lear.

INCIDENTS IN THE LIFE OF
MY UNCLE ARLY

I

OH! my aged Uncle Arly,
    Sitting on a heap of barley
        Through the silent hours of night,
Close beside a leafy thicket;
On his nose there was a cricket,
In his hat a Railway-Ticket,
    (But his shoes were far too tight.)

II

Long ago, in youth, he squander'd
All his goods away, and wander'd
    To the Timskoop-hills afar.

There on golden sunsets glazing
Every evening found him gazing,
    Singing, " Orb! you 're quite amazing!
    How I wonder what you are! "

III

Like the ancient Medes and Persians,
Always by his own exertions
    He subsisted on those hills;
Whiles, by teaching children spelling,
Or at times by merely yelling,
Or at intervals by selling
    " Propter's Nicodemus Pills."

IV

Later, in his morning rambles,
He perceived the moving brambles
    Something square and white disclose : —
'T was a First-class Railway-Ticket;
But on stooping down to pick it
Off the ground, a pea-green cricket
    Settled on my uncle's nose.

V

Never, nevermore, oh! never
Did that cricket leave him ever, —
    Dawn or evening, day or night;
Clinging as a constant treasure,
Chirping with a cheerious measure,
Wholly to my uncle's pleasure,
    (Though his shoes were far too tight.)

VI

So for three and forty winters,
Till his shoes were worn to splinters
    All those hills he wander'd o'er, —
Sometimes silent, sometimes yelling;
Till he came to Borley-Melling,
Near his old ancestral dwelling,
    (But his shoes were far too tight.)

VII

On a little heap of barley
Died my aged Uncle Arly,
    And they buried him one night
Close beside the leafy thicket;
There, his hat and Railway-Ticket;
There, his ever faithful cricket;
    (But his shoes were far too tight.)

Edward Lear.

LINES TO A YOUNG LADY

HOW pleasant to know Mr. Lear!"
    Who has written such volumes of stuff!
    Some think him ill-tempered and queer,
But a few think him pleasant enough.

His mind is concrete and fastidious,
    His nose is remarkably big;
His visage is more or less hideous,
    His beard it resembles a wig.

[88]

He has ears, and two eyes, and ten fingers,
  Leastways if you reckon two thumbs;
Long ago he was one of the singers,
  But now he is one of the dumbs.

He sits in a beautiful parlour,
  With hundreds of books on the wall;
He drinks a great deal of Marsala,
  But never gets tipsy at all.

He has many friends, laymen and clerical,
  Old Foss is the name of his cat:
His body is perfectly spherical,
  He weareth a runcible hat.

When he walks in a waterproof white,
  The children run after him so!
Calling out, " He's come out in his night-
  Gown, that crazy old Englishman, oh!"

He weeps by the side of the ocean,
  He weeps on the top of the hill;
He purchases pancakes and lotion,
  And chocolate shrimps from the mill.

He reads but he cannot speak Spanish,
  He cannot abide ginger-beer:
Ere the days of his pilgrimage vanish,
  How pleasant to know Mr. Lear.

                              Edward Lear.

WAYS AND MEANS

I'LL tell thee everything I can;
 There's little to relate.
 I saw an aged aged man,
  A-sitting on a gate.
"Who are you, aged man?" I said,
 "And how is it you live?"
His answer trickled through my head
 Like water through a sieve.

He said, "I look for butterflies
 That sleep among the wheat:
I make them into mutton-pies,
 And sell them in the street.
I sell them unto men," he said,
 "Who sail on stormy seas;
And that's the way I get my bread —
 A trifle, if you please."

But I was thinking of a plan
 To dye one's whiskers green,
And always use so large a fan
 That they could not be seen.
So, having no reply to give
 To what the old man said,
I cried, "Come, tell me how you live!"
 And thumped him on the head.

His accents mild took up the tale;
  He said, " I go my ways
And when I find a mountain-rill
  I set it in a blaze;
And thence they make a stuff they call
  Rowland's Macassar Oil —
Yet twopence-halfpenny is all
  They give me for my toil."

But I was thinking of a way
  To feed oneself on batter,
And so go on from day to day
  Getting a little fatter.
I shook him well from side to side,
  Until his face was blue;
" Come, tell me how you live," I cried,
  " And what it is you do ! "

He said, " I hunt for haddock's eyes
  Among the heather bright,
And work them into waistcoat-buttons
  In the silent night.
And these I do not sell for gold
  Or coin of silvery shine,
But for a copper halfpenny
  And that will purchase nine.

" I sometimes dig for buttered rolls,
  Or set limed twigs for crabs;
I sometimes search the grassy knolls
  For wheels of Hansom cabs.

And that 's the way " (he gave a wink)
" By which I get my wealth —
And very gladly will I drink
Your Honor's noble health."

I heard him then, for I had just
Completed my design
To keep the Menai Bridge from rust
By boiling it in wine.
I thanked him much for telling me
The way he got his wealth,
But chiefly for his wish that he
Might drink my noble health.

And now if e'er by chance I put
My fingers into glue,
Or madly squeeze a right-hand foot
Into a left-hand shoe,
Or if I drop upon my toe
A very heavy weight,
I weep, for it reminds me so
Of that old man I used to know —
Whose look was mild, whose speech was slow,
Whose hair was whiter than the snow,
Whose face was very like a crow,
With eyes, like cinders, all aglow,
Who seemed distracted with his woe,
Who rocked his body to and fro,
And muttered mumblingly, and low,
As if his mouth were full of dough,

Who snorted like a buffalo —
That summer evening, long ago,
A-sitting on a gate.

Lewis Carroll.

THE WALRUS AND THE
CARPENTER

THE sun was shining on the sea,
  Shining with all his might :
  He did his very best to make
The billows smooth and bright —
And this was odd, because it was
  The middle of the night.

The moon was shining sulkily,
  Because she thought the sun
Had got no business to be there
  After the day was done —
" It 's very rude of him," she said,
  " To come and spoil the fun ! "

The sea was wet as wet could be,
  The sands were dry as dry.
You could not see a cloud, because
  No cloud was in the sky :
No birds were flying overhead —
  There were no birds to fly.

The Walrus and the Carpenter
    Were walking close at hand;
They wept like anything to see
    Such quantities of sand :
" If this were only cleared away,"
    They said, " it would be grand ! "

" If seven maids with seven mops
    Swept it for half a year,
Do you suppose," the Walrus said,
    " That they could get it clear ? "
" I doubt it," said the Carpenter,
    And shed a bitter tear.

" O Oysters come and walk with us ! "
    The Walrus did beseech.
" A pleasant walk, a pleasant talk,
    Along the briny beach :
We cannot do with more than four,
    To give a hand to each."

The eldest Oyster looked at him,
    But not a word he said :
The eldest Oyster winked his eye,
    And shook his heavy head —
Meaning to say he did not choose
    To leave the oyster-bed.

But four young Oysters hurried up,
    All eager for the treat :
Their coats were brushed, their faces washed,

Their shoes were clean and neat —
And this was odd, because, you know,
They had n't any feet.

Four other Oysters followed them,
    And yet another four ;
And thick and fast they came at last,
    And more, and more, and more —
All hopping through the frothy waves,
    And scrambling to the shore.

The Walrus and the Carpenter
    Walked on a mile or so,
And then they rested on a rock
    Conveniently low :
And all the little Oysters stood
    And waited in a row.

" The time has come," the Walrus said,
    " To talk of many things :
Of shoes — and ships — and sealing-wax —
    Of cabbages — and kings —
And why the sea is boiling hot —
    And whether pigs have wings."

" But wait a bit," the Oysters cried,
    " Before we have our chat ;
For some of us are out of breath,
    And all of us are fat ! "
" No hurry ! " said the Carpenter.
    They thanked him much for that.

" A loaf of bread," the Walrus said,
  " Is what we chiefly need :
Pepper and vinegar besides
  Are very good indeed —
Now if you 're ready, Oysters dear,
  We can begin to feed."

" But not on us ! " the Oysters cried,
  Turning a little blue.
" After such kindness that would be
  A dismal thing to do ! "
" The night is fine," the Walrus said,
  " Do you admire the view ? "

" It was so kind of you to come !
  And you are very nice ! "
The Carpenter said nothing but
  " Cut us another slice :
I wish you were not quite so deaf —
  I 've had to ask you twice ! "

" It seems a shame," the Walrus said,
  " To play them such a trick,
After we 've brought them out so far,
  And made them trot so quick ! "
The Carpenter said nothing but
  " The butter 's spread too thick ! "

" I weep for you," the Walrus said ;
  " I deeply sympathize."
With sobs and tears he sorted out

Those of the largest size,
Holding his pocket-handkerchief
Before his streaming eyes.

"O Oysters," said the Carpenter,
"You 've had a pleasant run!
Shall we be trotting home again?"
But answer came there none—
And this was scarcely odd, because
They 'd eaten every one.

Lewis Carroll.

THE HUNTING OF THE SNARK

WE have sailed many months, we have sailed
many weeks,
(Four weeks to the month you may
mark),
But never as yet ('t is your Captain who speaks)
Have we caught the least glimpse of a Snark!

"We have sailed many weeks, we have sailed
many days,
(Seven days to the week I allow),
But a Snark, on the which we might lovingly gaze,
We have never beheld until now!

"Come, listen, my men, while I tell you again
The five unmistakable marks
By which you may know, wheresoever you go,
The warranted genuine Snarks.

"Let us take them in order. The first is the taste,
　　Which is meagre and hollow, but crisp :
Like a coat that is rather too tight in the waist,
　　With a flavour of Will-o-the-wisp.

"Its habit of getting up late you'll agree
　　That it carries too far, when I say
That it frequently breakfasts at five-o'clock tea,
　　And dines on the following day.

"The third is its slowness in taking a jest.
　　Should you happen to venture on one,
It will sigh like a thing that is greatly distressed ;
　　And it always looks grave at a pun.

"The fourth is its fondness for bathing-machines,
　　Which it constantly carries about,
And believes that they add to the beauty of scenes —
　　A sentiment open to doubt.

"The fifth is ambition. It next will be right
　　To describe each particular batch ;
Distinguishing those that have feathers, and bite,
　　From those that have whiskers, and scratch.

"For, although common Snarks do no manner of
　　　　harm,
　　Yet I feel it my duty to say
Some are Boojums —" The Bellman broke off
　　　　in alarm,
　　For the Baker had fainted away.

They roused him with muffins — they roused him
    with ice —
They roused him with mustard and cress —
They roused him with jam and judicious advice —
    They set him conundrums to guess.

When at length he sat up and was able to speak,
    His sad story he offered to tell;
And the Bellman cried, " Silence !   Not even a
    shriek ! "
    And excitedly tingled his bell.

"My father and mother were honest, though
    poor — "
  " Skip all that ! " cried the Bellman in haste,
" If it once becomes dark, there's no chance of a
    Snark,
    We have hardly a minute to waste ! "

" I skip forty years," said the Baker, in tears,
  " And proceed without further remark
To the day when you took me aboard of your ship
    To help you in hunting the Snark.

" You may seek it with thimbles — and seek it with
    care ;
    You may hunt it with forks and hope;
You may threaten its life with a railway-share;
    You may charm it with smiles and soap —

"I said it in Hebrew — I said it in Dutch —
    I said it in German and Greek;
But I wholly forgot (and it vexes me much)
    That English is what you speak!"

"The thing can be done," said the Butcher, "I
        think
    The thing must be done, I am sure.
The thing shall be done!   Bring me paper and ink,
    The best there is time to procure."

So engrossed was the Butcher, he heeded them not,
    As he wrote with a pen in each hand,
And explained all the while in a popular style
    Which the Beaver could well understand.

"Taking Three as the subject to reason about —
    A convenient number to state —
We add Seven and Ten and then multiply out
    By One Thousand diminished by Eight.

"The result we proceed to divide, as you see,
    By Nine Hundred and Ninety and Two;
Then subtract Seventeen, and the answer must be
    Exactly and perfectly true.

"As to temper, the Jubjub 's a desperate bird,
    Since it lives in perpetual passion :
Its taste in costume is entirely absurd —
    It is ages ahead of the fashion.

" Its flavor when cooked is more exquisite far
  Than mutton or oysters or eggs :
(Some think it keeps best in an ivory jar,
  And some, in mahogany kegs :)

" You boil it in sawdust ; you salt it in glue :
  You condense it with locusts and tape ;
Still keeping one principal object in view —
  To preserve its symmetrical shape."

The Butcher would gladly have talked till next day,
  But he felt that the Lesson must end,
And he wept with delight in attempting to say
  He considered the Beaver his friend.

Lewis Carroll.

SYLVIE AND BRUNO

HE thought he saw a Banker's clerk
      Descending from the 'bus ;
    He looked again, and found it was
  A Hippopotamus.
" If this should stay to dine," he said,
  " There won't be much for us ! "

He thought he saw an Albatross
  That fluttered round the lamp :
He looked again, and found it was
  A Penny-Postage-Stamp.
" You 'd best be getting home," he said ;
  " The nights are very damp ! "

[101]

He thought he saw a Coach-and-Four
That stood beside his bed:
He looked again, and found it was
A Bear without a Head.
" Poor thing," he said, " poor silly thing!
It 's waiting to be fed ! "

He thought he saw a Kangaroo
That worked a coffee-mill:
He looked again, and found it was
A Vegetable-Pill.
" Were I to swallow this," he said,
" I should be very ill ! "

He thought he saw a Rattlesnake
That questioned him in Greek:
He looked again, and found it was
The Middle of Next Week.
" The one thing I regret," he said,
" Is that it cannot speak ! "

Lewis Carroll.

GENTLE ALICE BROWN

IT was a robber's daughter, and her name was
    Alice Brown.
    Her father was the terror of a small Italian
    town;
Her mother was a foolish, weak, but amiable old
    thing;
But it is n't of her parents that I 'm going for to sing.

As Alice was a-sitting at her window-sill one day,
A beautiful young gentleman he chanced to pass
 that way;
She cast her eyes upon him, and he looked so good
 and true,
That she thought, "I could be happy with a gentleman like you!"

And every morning passed her house that cream
 of gentlemen,
She knew she might expect him at a quarter unto
 ten,
A sorter in the Custom-house, it was his daily road
(The Custom-house was fifteen minutes' walk from
 her abode.)

But Alice was a pious girl, who knew it was n't
 wise
To look at strange young sorters with expressive
 purple eyes;
So she sought the village priest to whom her
 family confessed,
The priest by whom their little sins were carefully
 assessed.

"Oh, holy father," Alice said, "'t would grieve
 you, would it not?
To discover that I was a most disreputable lot!
Of all unhappy sinners I 'm the most unhappy
 one!"
The padre said, "Whatever have you been and
 gone and done?"

"I have helped mamma to steal a little kiddy
from its dad,
I've assisted dear papa in cutting up a little lad.
I've planned a little burglary and forged a little
check,
And slain a little baby for the coral on its neck!"

The worthy pastor heaved a sigh, and dropped a
silent tear —
And said, "You must n't judge yourself too heavily,
my dear —
It 's wrong to murder babies, little corals for to
fleece;
But sins like these one expiates at half-a-crown
apiece.

"Girls will be girls — you 're very young, and
flighty in your mind;
Old heads upon young shoulders we must not expect to find:
We must n't be too hard upon these little girlish
tricks —
Let 's see — five crimes at half-a-crown — exactly
twelve-and-six."

"Oh, father," little Alice cried, "your kindness
makes me weep,
You do these little things for me so singularly
cheap —
Your thoughtful liberality I never can forget;
But O there is another crime I have n't mentioned
yet!

"A pleasant-looking gentleman, with pretty purple
   eyes,
I 've noticed at my window, as I 've sat a-catching
   flies;
He passes by it every day as certain as can be—
I blush to say I 've winked at him and he has
   winked at me!"

"For shame," said Father Paul, "my erring
   daughter! On my word
This is the most distressing news that I have ever
   heard.
Why, naughty girl, your excellent papa has pledged
   your hand
To a promising young robber, the lieutenant of
   his band!

"This dreadful piece of news will pain your worthy
   parents so!
They are the most remunerative customers I know;
For many many years they 've kept starvation from
   my doors,
I never knew so criminal a family as yours!

"The common country folk in this insipid neighborhood
Have nothing to confess, they 're so ridiculously
   good;
And if you marry any one respectable at all,
Why, you 'll reform, and what will then become
   of Father Paul?"

The worthy priest, he up and drew his cowl upon
  his crown,
And started off in haste to tell the news to Robber
  Brown;
To tell him how his daughter, who now was for
  marriage fit,
Had winked upon a sorter, who reciprocated it.

Good Robber Brown, he muffled up his anger
  pretty well,
He said, " I have a notion, and that notion I will
  tell;
I will nab this gay young sorter, terrify him into
  fits,
And get my gentle wife to chop him into little bits.

" I 've studied human nature, and I know a thing
  or two,
Though a girl may fondly love a living gent, as
  many do —
A feeling of disgust upon her senses there will fall
When she looks upon his body chopped particularly
  small."

He traced that gallant sorter to a still suburban
  square;
He watched his opportunity and seized him unaware;
He took a life-preserver and he hit him on the
  head,
And Mrs. Brown dissected him before she went to
  bed.

And pretty little Alice grew more settled in her
mind,
She nevermore was guilty of a weakness of the
kind,
Until at length good Robber Brown bestowed her
pretty hand
On the promising young robber, the lieutenant of
his band.

W. S. Gilbert.

THE STORY OF PRINCE AGIB

STRIKE the concertina's melancholy string!
Blow the spirit-stirring harp like any thing!
Let the piano's martial blast
Rouse the Echoes of the Past,
For of Agib, Prince of Tartary, I sing!

Of Agib, who amid Tartaric scenes,
Wrote a lot of ballet-music in his teens:
His gentle spirit rolls
In the melody of souls —
Which is pretty, but I don't know what it means.

Of Agib, who could readily, at sight,
Strum a march upon the loud Theodolite:
He would diligently play
On the Zoetrope all day,
And blow the gay Pantechnicon all night.

[107]

One winter — I am shaky in my dates —
Came two starving minstrels to his gates,
  Oh, Allah be obeyed,
  How infernally they played!
I remember that they called themselves the "Oiiaits."

Oh! that day of sorrow, misery, and rage,
I shall carry to the Catacombs of Age,
  Photographically lined
  On the tablet of my mind,
When a yesterday has faded from its page!

Alas! Prince Agib went and asked them in!
Gave them beer, and eggs, and sweets, and scents,
  and tin.
  And when (as snobs would say)
  They " put it all away,"
He requested them to tune up and begin.

Though its icy horror chill you to the core,
I will tell you what I never told before,
  The consequences true
  Of that awful interview,
For I listened at the key-hole in the door!

They played him a sonata — let me see!
" *Medulla oblongata* " — key of G.
  Then they began to sing
  That extremely lovely thing,
" Scherzando! ma non troppo, ppp."

He gave them money, more than they could
        count,
Scent, from a most ingenious little fount,
        More beer, in little kegs,
        Many dozen hard-boiled eggs,
And goodies to a fabulous amount.

Now follows the dim horror of my tale,
And I feel I'm growing gradually pale,
        For, even at this day,
        Though its sting has passed away,
When I venture to remember it, I quail!

The elder of the brothers gave a squeal,
All-overish it made me for to feel!
        " Oh Prince," he says, says he,
        " *If a Prince indeed you be*,
I've a mystery I'm going to reveal!

" Oh, listen, if you'd shun a horrid death,
To what the gent who's speaking to you, saith:
        No ' Oiiaits' in truth are we,
        As you fancy that we be,
For (ter-remble) I am Aleck — this is Beth!"

Said Agib, " Oh! accursed of your kind,
I have heard that you are men of evil mind!"
        Beth gave a dreadful shriek —
        But before he'd time to speak
I was mercilessly collared from behind.

[109]

In number ten or twelve or even more,
They fastened me, full length upon the floor.
    On my face extended flat
    I was walloped with a cat
For listening at the key-hole of the door.

Oh! the horror of that agonizing thrill!
(I can feel the place in frosty weather still).
    For a week from ten to four
    I was fastened to the floor,
While a mercenary wopped me with a will!

They branded me, and broke me on a wheel,
And they left me in an hospital to heal;
    And, upon my solemn word,
    I have never never heard
What those Tartars had determined to reveal.

But that day of sorrow, misery, and rage,
I shall carry to the Catacombs of Age,
    Photographically lined
    On the tablet of my mind,
When a yesterday has faded from its page!

                                    W. S. Gilbert.

FERDINANDO AND ELVIRA, OR
THE GENTLE PIEMAN

L OVE you?" said I, then I sighed, and then
        I gazed upon her sweetly —
    For I think I do this sort of thing particu-
        larly neatly —

" Tell me whither I may hie me, tell me, dear
    one, that I may know —
Is it up the highest Andes? down a horrible
    volcano? "

But she said, " It is n't polar bears, or hot vol-
    canic grottoes,
Only find out who it is that writes those lovely
    cracker mottoes."

Seven weary years I wandered — Patagonia, China,
    Norway,
Till at last I sank exhausted, at a pastrycook his
    doorway.

And he chirped and sang and skipped about, and
    laughed with laughter hearty,
He was wonderfully active for so very stout a
    party.

And I said, " Oh, gentle pieman, why so very, very
    merry?
Is it purity of conscience, or your one-and-seven
    sherry? "
    . . . .

" Then I polish all the silver which a supper-table
    lacquers;
Then I write the pretty mottoes which you find
    inside the crackers."

"Found at last!" I madly shouted. "Gentle
  pieman, you astound me!"
Then I waved the turtle soup enthusiastically
  round me.

And I shouted and I danced until he'd quite a
  crowd around him,
And I rushed away, exclaiming, "I have found
  him! I have found him!"

                                        W. S. Gilbert.

GENERAL JOHN

THE bravest names for fire and flames,
    And all that mortal durst,
    Were General John and Private James,
Of the Sixty-seventy-first.

General John was a soldier tried,
    A chief of warlike dons;
A haughty stride and a withering pride
    Were Major-General John.

A sneer would play on his martial phiz,
    Superior birth to show;
" Pish!" was a favorite word of his,
    And he often said " Ho! ho!"

Full-Private James described might be,
    As a man of mournful mind;
No characteristic trait had he
    Of any distinctive kind.

From the ranks, one day, cried Private James,
  " Oh ! Major-General John,
I 've doubts of our respective names,
  My mournful mind upon.

" A glimmering thought occurs to me,
  (Its source I can't unearth),
But I 've a kind of notion we
  Were cruelly changed at birth.

" I 've a strange idea, each other's names
  That we have each got on.
Such things have been," said Private James.
  " They have ! " sneered General John.

" My General John, I swear upon
  My oath I think it is so — "
" Pish ! " proudly sneered his General John,
  And he also said " Ho ! ho ! "

" My General John ! my General John !
  My General John ! " quoth he,
" This aristocratical sneer upon
  Your face I blush to see.

" No truly great or generous cove
  Deserving of them names
Would sneer at a fixed idea that 's drove
  In the mind of a Private James ! "

Said General John, " Upon your claims
    No need your breath to waste ;
If this is a joke, Full-Private James,
    It 's a joke of doubtful taste.

" But being a man of doubtless worth,
    If you feel certain quite
That we were probably changed at birth,
    I 'll venture to say you 're right."

So General John as Private James
    Fell in, parade upon ;
And Private James, by change of names,
    Was Major-General John.

                          W. S. Gilbert.

LITTLE BILLEE

THERE were three sailors of Bristol City
    Who took a boat and went to sea,
    But first with beef and captain's biscuits,
And pickled pork they loaded she.

There was gorging Jack, and guzzling Jimmy,
    And the youngest he was little Billee.
Now when they 'd got as far as the Equator,
    They 'd nothing left but one split pea.

Says gorging Jack to guzzling Jimmy,
  " I am extremely hungaree."
To gorging Jack says guzzling Jimmy,
  " We 've nothing left, us must eat we."

Says gorging Jack to guzzling Jimmy,
  " With one another we should n't agree !
There 's little Bill, he 's young and tender,
  We 're old and tough, so let 's eat he."

" O Billy ! we 're going to kill and eat you,
  So undo the button of your chemie."
When Bill received this information,
  He used his pocket-handkerchie.

" First let me say my catechism,
  Which my poor mother taught to me."
" Make haste ! make haste !" says guzzling Jimmy,
  While Jack pulled out his snicker-snee.

Then Bill went up to the main-top-gallant-mast,
  And down he fell on his bended knee,
He scarce had come to the Twelfth Commandment,
  When up he jumps — " There 's land I see !"

" Jerusalem and Madagascar,
  And North and South Amerikee,
There 's the British flag a-riding at anchor,
  With Admiral Napier, K.C.B."

So when they got aboard of the Admiral's,
    He hanged fat Jack and flogged Jimmee,
But as for little Bill, he made him
    The captain of a Seventy-three.

                      W. M. Thackeray.

THE WRECK OF THE "JULIE PLANTE" *

ON wan dark night on Lac St. Pierre,
    De win' she blow, blow, blow,
    An' de crew of de wood scow "Julie Plante"
Got scar't an' run below —
For de win' she blow lak hurricane;
    Bimeby she blow some more,
An' de scow bus' up on Lac St. Pierre
    Wan arpent from de shore.

De captinne walk on de fronte deck,
    An' walk de hin' deck too —
He call de crew from up de hole,
    He call de cook also.
De cook she 's name was Rosie,
    She come from Montreal,
Was chambre maid on lumber barge,
    On de Grande Lachine Canal.

    * By permission of G. P. Putnam's Sons; from "The Habitant," copyright, 1897.

                [116]

De win' she blow from nor'-eas'-wes', —
    De sout' win' she blow too,
W'en Rosie cry, " Mon cher captinne,
    Mon cher, w'at I shall do ? "
Den de captinne t'row de big ankerre,
    But still de scow she dreef,
De crew he can't pass on de shore,
    Becos he los' hees skeef.

De night was dark lak wan black cat,
    De wave run high an' fas',
W'en de captinne tak' de Rosie girl
    An' tie her to de mas'.
Den he also tak' de life preserve,
    An' jomp off on de lak',
An' say, " Good-by, ma Rosie dear,
    I go down for your sak'."

Nex' morning very early
    'Bout ha'f-pas' two — t'ree — four —
De captinne — scow — an' de poor Rosie
    Was corpses on de shore.
For de win' she blow lak' hurricane,
    Bimeby she blow some more,
An' de scow, bus' up on Lac St. Pierre,
    Wan arpent from de shore.

MORAL

Now all good wood scow sailor man
    Tak' warning by dat storm
An' go an' marry some nice French girl
    An' live on wan beeg farm.

[117]

De win' can blow lak' hurricane
    An' s'pose she blow some more,
You can't get drown on Lac St. Pierre
    So long you stay on shore.

                   William H. Drummond.

THE SHIPWRECK

UPON the poop the captain stands,
    As starboard as may be;
    And pipes on deck the topsail hands
To reef the topsail-gallant strands
    Across the briny sea.

" Ho! splice the anchor under-weigh! "
    The captain loudly cried;
" Ho! lubbers brave, belay! belay!
For we must luff for Falmouth Bay
    Before to-morrow's tide."

The good ship was a racing yawl,
    A spare-rigged schooner sloop,
Athwart the bows the taffrails all
In grummets gay appeared to fall,
    To deck the mainsail poop.

But ere they made the Foreland Light,
    And Deal was left behind,
The wind it blew great gales that night,
And blew the doughty captain tight,
    Full three sheets in the wind.

And right across the tiller head
   The horse it ran apace,
Whereon a traveller hitched and sped
Along the jib and vanished
   To heave the trysail brace.

What ship could live in such a sea?
   What vessel bear the shock?
"Ho! starboard port your helm-a-lee!
Ho! reef the maintop-gallant-tree,
   With many a running block!"

And right upon the Scilly Isles
   The ship had run aground;
When lo! the stalwart Captain Giles
Mounts up upon the gaff and smiles,
   And slews the compass round.

"Saved! saved!" with joy the sailors cry,
   And scandalize the skiff;
As taut and hoisted high and dry
They see the ship unstoppered lie
   Upon the sea-girt cliff.

And since that day in Falmouth Bay,
   As herring-fishers trawl,
The younkers hear the boatswains say
How Captain Giles that awful day
   Preserved the sinking yawl.

                E. H. Palmer.

A SAILOR'S YARN *

As narrated by the second mate to one of the marines.

THIS is the tale that was told to me,
 By a battered and shattered son of the sea:
 To me and my messmate, Silas Green,
When I was a guileless young marine.

" 'T was the good ship ' Gyacutus,'
All in the China seas;
With the wind a lee, and the capstan free,
To catch the summer breeze.

" 'T was Captain Porgie on the deck
To the mate in the mizzen hatch,
While the boatswain bold, in the for'ard hold,
Was winding his larboard watch.

" ' Oh, how does our good ship head to-night?
How heads our gallant craft ? '
' Oh, she heads to the E. S. W. by N.
And the binnacle lies abaft.'

" ' Oh, what does the quadrant indicate?
And how does the sextant stand ? '
' Oh, the sextant 's down to the freezing point
And the quadrant 's lost a hand.'

 * By permission of Houghton, Mifflin & Co. ; from " Ballads of Blue Water," copyright, 1895.

" ' Oh, if the quadrant 's lost a hand,
And the sextant falls so low,
It 's our body and bones to Davy Jones
This night are bound to go.

" ' Oh, fly aloft to the garboard-strake,
And reef the spanker boom,
Bend a stubbing sail on the martingale
To give her weather room.

" ' Oh, boatswain, down in the for'ard hold
What water do you find ? '
' Four foot and a half by the royal gaff
And rather more behind.'

" ' Oh, sailors, collar your marline spikes
And each belaying pin ;
Come, stir your stumps to spike the pumps,
Or more will be coming in.'

" ' They stirred their stumps, they spiked the pumps
They spliced the mizzen brace ;
Aloft and alow they worked, but, oh !
The water gained apace.

" They bored a hole below her line
To let the water out,
But more and more with awful roar
The water in did spout.

" Then up spoke the cook of our gallant ship —
And he was a lubber brave —
' I 've several wives in various ports,
And my life I 'd like to save.'

" Then up spoke the captain of marines,
Who dearly loved his prog:
' It 's awful to die, and it 's worse to be dry,
And I move we pipes to grog.'

" Oh, then 't was the gallant second-mate
As stopped them sailors' jaw,
'T was the second-mate whose hand had weight
In laying down the law.

" He took the anchor on his back,
And leapt into the main;
Through foam and spray he clove his way,
And sunk, and rose again.

" Through foam and spray a league away
The anchor stout he bore,
Till, safe at last, I made it fast,
And warped the ship ashore."

This is the tale that was told to me,
By that modest and truthful son of the sea.
And I envy the life of a second mate,
Though captains curse him and sailors hate;
For he ain't like some of the swabs I 've seen,
As would go and lie to a poor marine.

J. J. Roche.

THE WALLOPING WINDOW-BLIND *

A CAPITAL ship for an ocean trip
    Was the " Walloping Window-blind " —
    No gale that blew dismayed her crew
Or troubled the captain's mind.
The man at the wheel was taught to feel
    Contempt for the wildest blow,
And it often appeared, when the weather had
    cleared,
    That he 'd been in his bunk below.

The boatswain's mate was very sedate,
    Yet fond of amusement, too ;
And he played hop-scotch with the starboard watch,
    While the captain tickled the crew.
And the gunner we had was apparently mad,
    For he sat on the after rail,
And fired salutes with the captain's boots,
    In the teeth of the booming gale.

The captain sat in a commodore's hat
    And dined in a royal way
On toasted pigs and pickles and figs
    And gummery bread each day.
But the cook was Dutch and behaved as such :
    For the food that he gave the crew
Was a number of tons of hot-cross buns
    Chopped up with sugar and glue.

* By permission of the author ; from " Davy and the Goblin,"
copyright, 1884, 1885, by the Century Co. ; 1885, by Ticknor & Co.

And we all felt ill as mariners will,
  On a diet that's cheap and rude;
And we shivered and shook as we dipped the cook
  In a tub of his gluesome food.
Then nautical pride we laid aside,
  And we cast the vessel ashore
On the Gulliby Isles, where the Poohpooh smiles,
  And the Anagazanders roar.

Composed of sand was that favored land,
  And trimmed with cinnamon straws;
And pink and blue was the pleasing hue
  Of the Tickletoeteaser's claws.
And we sat on the edge of a sandy ledge
  And shot at the whistling bee;
And the Binnacle-bats wore water-proof hats
  As they danced in the sounding sea.

On rubagub bark, from dawn to dark,
  We fed, till we all had grown
Uncommonly shrunk, — when a Chinese junk
  Came by from the torriby zone.
She was stubby and square, but we did n't much care,
  And we cheerily put to sea;
And we left the crew of the junk to chew
  The bark of the rubagub tree.

Charles E. Carryl.

THE ROLLICKING MASTODON *

A ROLLICKING Mastodon lived in Spain,
   In the trunk of a Tranquil Tree.
   His face was plain, but his jocular vein
Was a burst of the wildest glee.
His voice was strong and his laugh so long
   That people came many a mile,
And offered to pay a guinea a day
   For the fractional part of a smile.

   The Rollicking Mastodon's laugh was wide —
      Indeed, 't was a matter of family pride;
   And oh! so proud of his jocular vein
      Was the Rollicking Mastodon over in Spain.

The Rollicking Mastodon said one day,
   " I feel that I need some air,
For a little ozone 's a tonic for bones,
   As well as a gloss for the hair."
So he skipped along and warbled a song
   In his own triumphulant way.
His smile was bright and his skip was light
   As he chirruped his roundelay.

   The Rollicking Mastodon tripped along,
      And sang what Mastodons call a song;
   But every note of it seemed to pain
      The Rollicking Mastodon over in Spain.

* By permission of Lothrop Publishing Company; from " Wide Awake," copyright.

A Little Peetookle came over the hill,
  Dressed up in a bollitant coat;
And he said, " You need some harroway seed,
  And a little advice for your throat."
The Mastodon smiled and said, " My child,
  There 's a chance for your taste to grow.
If you polish your mind, you 'll certainly find
  How little, how little you know."

    The Little Peetookle, his teeth he ground
      At the Mastodon's singular sense of sound;
    For he felt it a sort of a musical stain
      On the Rollicking Mastodon over in Spain.

Alas! and alas! has it come to this pass?"
  Said the Little Peetookle. "Dear me!
It certainly seems your horrible screams
  Intended for music must be!"
The Mastodon stopped, his ditty he dropped,
  And murmured, " Good morning, my dear!
I never will sing to a sensitive thing
  That shatters a song with a sneer!"

    The Rollicking Mastodon bade him " adieu."
      Of course 't was a sensible thing to do;
    For Little Peetookle is spared the strain
      Of the Rollicking Mastodon over in Spain.

                                   Arthur Macy.

THE SILVER QUESTION *

THE Sun appeared so smug and bright,
   One day, that I made bold
   To ask him what he did each night
With all his surplus gold.

He flushed uncomfortably red,
   And would not meet my eye.
" I travel round the world," he said,
   " And travelling rates are high."

With frigid glance I pierced him through.
   He squirmed and changed his tune.
Said he : " I will be frank with you :
   I lend it to the Moon.

" Poor thing!   You know she 's growing old
   And has n't any folk.
She suffers terribly from cold,
   And half the time she 's broke."

   .   .   .   .   .   .

That evening on the beach I lay
   Behind a lonely dune,
And as she rose above the bay
   I buttonholed the Moon.

" Tell me about that gold," said I.
   I saw her features fall.
" You see, it 's useless to deny ;
   The Sun has told me all."

"Sir!" she exclaimed, "how *can* you try
    An honest Moon this way?
As for the gold, I put it by
    Against a rainy day."

I smiled and shook my head. "All right,
    If you *must* know," said she,
"I change it into silver bright
    Wherewith to tip the Sea.

"He is so faithful and so good,
    A most deserving case;
If he should leave, I fear it would
    Be hard to fill his place."
    .   .   .   .   .   .

When asked if they accepted tips,
    The waves became so rough;
I thought of those at sea in ships,
    And felt I'd said enough.

For if one virtue I have learned,
    'T is *tact;* so I forbore
To press the matter, though I burned
    To ask one question more.

I hate a scene, and do not wish
    To be mixed up in gales,
But, oh, I longed to ask the Fish
    Whence came their silver scales!

                    Oliver Herford.

THE SINGULAR SANGFROID OF
BABY BUNTING *

BARTHOLOMEW Benjamin Bunting
　　Had only three passions in life,
　And one of the trio was hunting,
　　The others his babe and his wife.
And always, so rigid his habits,
　He frolicked at home until two,
And then started hunting for rabbits,
　And hunted till fall of the dew.

Belinda Bellonia Bunting,
　　Thus widowed for half of the day,
Her duty maternal confronting,
　　With baby would patiently play.
When thus was her energy wasted,
　A patented food she'd dispense.
(She had bought it the day that they pasted
　The posters all over her fence.)

But Bonaparte Buckingham Bunting,
　　The infant thus blindly adored,
Replied to her worship by grunting,
　　Which showed he was brutally bored.
'T was little he cared for the troubles
　Of life.　Like a crab on the sands,
From his sweet little mouth he blew bubbles,
　And threatened the air with his hands.

---

* By permission of Harper & Brothers ; from " Mother Goose for
Grown-ups," copyright, 1900.

Bartholomew Benjamin Bunting
   One night, as his wife let him in,
Produced as the fruit of his hunting
   A cottontail's velvety skin,
Which, seeing young Bonaparte wriggle,
   He gave him without a demur,
And the babe with an aqueous giggle
   He swallowed the whole of the fur!

Belinda Bellonia Bunting
   Behaved like a consummate loon:
Her offspring in frenzy confronting
   She screamed herself mottled maroon:
She felt of his vertebræ spinal,
   Expecting he'd surely succumb,
And gave him one vigorous, final,
   Hard prod in the pit of his tum.

But Bonaparte Buckingham Bunting,
   At first but a trifle perplexed,
By a change in his manner of grunting
   Soon showed he was horribly vexed.
He displayed not a sign of repentance
   But spoke, in a dignified tone,
The only consecutive sentence
   He uttered. 'Twas: " Lemme alone."

The Moral: The parent that uses
   Precaution his folly regrets:
An infant gets all that he chooses,
   An infant chews all that he gets.

And colics? He constantly has 'em
  So long as his food is the best,
But he 'll swallow with never a spasm
  What ostriches could n't digest.

               Guy Wetmore Carryl.

FAITHLESS NELLY GRAY

BEN BATTLE was a soldier bold,
  And used to war's alarms:
  But a cannon-ball took off his legs,
So he laid down his arms!

Now, as they bore him off the field,
  Said he, "Let others shoot,
For here I leave my second leg,
  And the Forty-second Foot!"

The army surgeons made him limbs:
  Said he, "They 're only pegs;
But there 's as wooden members quite,
  As represent my legs!"

Now Ben he loved a pretty maid,
  Her name was Nelly Gray;
So he went to pay her his devours
  When he 'd devoured his pay!

But when he called on Nelly Gray,
    She made him quite a scoff;
And when she saw his wooden legs,
    Began to take them off!

" O Nelly Gray! O Nelly Gray!
    Is this your love so warm?
The love that loves a scarlet coat,
    Should be more uniform!"

Said she, " I loved a soldier once,
    For he was blithe and brave;
But I will never have a man
    With both legs in the grave!

" Before you had those timber toes,
    Your love I did allow,
But then you know, you stand upon
    Another footing now!"

" O Nelly Gray! O Nelly Gray!
    For all your jeering speeches,
At duty's call I left my legs
    In Badajos's breaches!"

" Why, then," said she, "you've lost the feet
    Of legs in war's alarms,
And now you cannot wear your shoes
    Upon your feats of arms!"

" Oh, false and fickle Nelly Gray;
    I know why you refuse :
Though I 've no feet — some other man
    Is standing in my shoes !

" I wish I ne'er had seen your face ;
    But now a long farewell !
For you will be my death — alas !
    You will not be my Nell ! "

Now, when he went from Nelly Gray,
    His heart so heavy got —
And life was such a burden grown,
    It made him take a knot !

So round his melancholy neck
    A rope he did entwine,
And, for his second time in life
    Enlisted in the Line !

One end he tied around a beam,
    And then removed his pegs,
And as his legs were off, — of course,
    He soon was off his legs !

And there he hung till he was dead
    As any nail in town, —
For though distress had cut him up,
    It could not cut him down !

A dozen men sat on his corpse,
  To find out why he died —
And they buried Ben in four cross-roads,
  With a stake in his inside !

Thomas Hood.

THE ELDERLY GENTLEMAN

BY the side of a murmuring stream an elderly
      gentleman sat.
  On the top of his head was a wig, and a-top
    of his wig was his hat.

The wind it blew high and blew strong, as the
    elderly gentleman sat;
And bore from his head in a trice, and plunged in
    the river his hat.

The gentleman then took his cane which lay by
    his side as he sat ;
And he dropped in the river his wig, in attempting
    to get out his hat.

His breast it grew cold with despair, and full in his
    eye madness sat ;
So he flung in the river his cane to swim with his
    wig, and his hat.

Cool reflection at last came across while this
    elderly gentleman sat ;
So he thought he would follow the stream and look
    for his cane, wig, and hat.

His head being thicker than common, o'er-balanced
    the rest of his fat;
And in plumped this son of a woman to follow his
    wig, cane, and hat.

George Canning.

MALUM OPUS

PROPE ripam fluvii solus
    A senex silently sat;
      Super capitum ecce his wig,
Et wig super, ecce his hat.

Blew Zephyrus alte, acerbus,
    Dum elderly gentleman sat;
Et a capite took up quite torve
    Et in rivum projecit his hat.

Tunc soft maledixit the old man,
    Tunc stooped from the bank where he sat
Et cum scipio poked in the water,
    Conatus servare his hat.

Blew Zephyrus alte, acerbus,
    The moment it saw him at that;
Et whisked his novum scratch wig
    In flumen, along with his hat.

Ab imo pectore damnavit
In cœruleus eye dolor sat;
Tunc despairingly threw in his cane
Nare cum his wig and his hat.

L'ENVOI

Contra bonos mores, don't swear
It 'est wicked you know (verbum sat),
Si this tale habet no other moral
Mehercle! You 're gratus to that!

James Appleton Morgan.

ÆSTIVATION *

IN candent ire the solar splendor flames;
The foles, languescent, pend from arid rames;
His humid front the cive, anheling, wipes,
And dreams of erring on ventiferous ripes.

How dulce to vive occult to mortal eyes,
Dorm on the herb with none to supervise,
Carp the suave berries from the crescent vine,
And bibe the flow from longicaudate kine.

To me also, no verdurous visions come
Save you exiguous pool's confervascum, —
No concave vast repeats the tender hue
That laves my milk-jug with celestial blue.

* By permission of Houghton, Mifflin & Co., authorized publishers.

Me wretched ! Let me curr to quercine shades !
Effund your albid hausts, lactiferous maids !
Oh, might I vole to some umbrageous chump, —
Depart, — be off, — excede, — evade, — erump !

O. W. Holmes.

A HOLIDAY TASK

Air — Jullien's Polka

QUI nunc dancere vult modo
    Wants to dance in the fashion, oh !
    Discere debet — ought to know,
Kickere floor cum heel et toe
      One, two three,
      Hop with me,
Whirligig, twirligig, rapidè.

Polkam jungere, Virgo, vis,
Will you join the Polka, Miss ?
Liberius — most willingly.
Sic agimus — then let us try :
      Nunc vide
      Skip with me,
Whirlabout, roundabout, celerè.

Tum lævâ citò, tum dextrâ
First to the left, and then t' other way ;
Aspice retrò in vultu,
You look at her, and she looks at you.

Das palmam,
Change hands ma'am
Celerè — run away, just in sham.

Gilbert Abbott à Becket.

PUER EX JERSEY

PUER ex Jersey
   Iens ad school;
    Vidit in meadow,
Infestum mule.

Ille approaches
O magnus sorrow!
Puer it skyward.
Funus ad morrow.

MORAL

Qui vidit a thing
Non ei well-known,
Est bene for him
Relinqui id alone.

Anonymous.

THE LITTLE PEACH

UNE petite pêche dans un orchard fleurit,
   Attendez à mon narration triste!
   Une petite pêche verdante fleurit.
Grâce à chaleur de soleil, et moisture de miste.
Il fleurit, il fleurit,
   Attendez à mon narration triste!

[138]

Signes dures pour les deux,
Petit Jean et sa sœur Sue,
Et la pêche d'une verdante hue,
Qui fleurit, qui fleurit,
Attendez à mon narration triste!

Anonymous.

MONSIEUR McGINTÉ

MONSIEUR McGinté allait en bas jusqu'au
          fond du mer,
     Ils ne l'ont pas encore trouvé
Je crois qu'il est certainement mouillé.
Monsieur McGinté, je le repéte, allait jusqu'au
     fond du mer,
     Habillé dans sa meilleure costume.

Anonymous.

YE LAYE OF YE WOODPECKORE

Picus Erythrocephalus :

O WHITHER goest thou, pale studént
          Within the wood so fur?
          Art on the chokesome cherry bent?
     Dost seek the chestnut burr?

[139]

Pale Studént.

O it is not for the mellow chestnút
That I so far am come,
Nor yet for puckery cherries, but
For Cypripediúm.

A blossom hangs the choke-cherry
And eke the chestnut burr,
And thou a silly fowl must be,
Thou red-head wood-peckér.

Picus Erythrocephalus :

Turn back, turn back, thou pale studént,
Nor in the forest go;
There lurks beneath his bosky tent
The deadly mosquitó,

And there the wooden-chuck doth tread,
And from the oak-tree's top
The red, red squirrels on thy head
The frequent acorn drop.

Pale Studént.

The wooden-chuck is next of kin
Unto the wood-peckér :
I fear not thine ill-boding din,
And why should I fear her ?

What though a score of acorns drop
  And squirrels' fur be red !
'T is not so ruddy as thy top —
  So scarlet as thy head.

O rarely blooms the Cypripe-
  diúm upon its stalk ;
And like a torch it shines to me
  Adown the dark wood-walk.

O joy to pluck it from the ground,
  To view the purple sac,
To touch the sessile stigma's round —
  And shall I then turn back ?

Picus Erythrocephalus :

O black and shining is the log
  That feeds the sumptuous weed,
Nor stone is found nor bedded log
  Where foot may well proceed.

Midmost it glimmers in the mire
  Like Jack o' Lanthorn's spark,
Lighting, with phosphorescent fire,
  The green umbrageous dark.

There while thy thirsty glances drink
  The fair and baneful plant,
Thy shoon within the ooze shall sink
  And eke thine either pant.

Pale Studént.

> Give o'er, give o'er, thou wood-peckóre;
>   The bark upon the tree,
> Thou, at thy will, mayst peck and bore
>   But peck and bore not me.
>
> Full two long hours I 've searched about
>   And 't would in sooth be rum,
> If I should now go back without
>   The Cypripediúm.

Picus Erythrocephalus :

> Farewell ! Farewell ! But this I tell
>   To thee, thou pale studént,
> Ere dews have fell, thou 'lt rue it well
>   That woodward thou didst went :
>
> Then whilst thou blows the drooping nose
>   And wip'st the pensive eye —
> There where the sad *symplocarpus fœtidus* grows,
>   Then think — O think of I !
>
> Loud flouted there that student wight
>   Solche warnynge for to hear ;
> " I scorn, old hen, thy threats of might,
>   And eke thine ill grammére.
>
> " Go peck the lice (or green or red)
>   That swarm the bass-wood tree,
> But wag no more thine addled head
>   Nor clack thy tongue at me."

[142]

The wood-peck turned to whet her beak,
　　The student heard her drum,
As through the wood he went to seek
　　The Cypripedíum.

Alas! and for that pale studént:
　　The evening bell did ring,
And down the walk the Freshmen went
　　Unto the prayer-meetíng;

Upon the fence loud rose the song,
　　The weak, weak tea was o'er —
Ha! who is he that sneaks along
　　Into South Middle's door?

The mud was on his shoon, and O!
　　The briar was in his thumb,
His staff was in his hand but no —
　　No Cypripedíum.

　　　　　　　　　　　Henry A. Beers.

COLLUSION BETWEEN A ALE-GAITER AND A WATER-SNAIK

THERE is a niland on a river lying,
　　Which runs into Gautimaly, a warm country,
　　Lying near the Tropicks, covered with sand;
Hear and their a symptum of a Wilow,
Hanging of its umberagious limbs & branches
Over the clear streme meandering far below.
This was the home of the now silent Alegaiter,

When not in his other element confine'd :
Here he wood set upon his eggs asleep
With 1 ey observant of flis and other passing
Objects : a while it kept a going on so :
Fereles of danger was the happy Alegaiter !
But a las ! in a nevil our Le was fourced to
Wake ! that dreme of Blis was two sweet for him.
1 morning the sun arose with unusool splender
Whitch allso did our Alegaiter, coming from the
        water,
His scails a flinging of the rais of the son back,
To the fountain-head which tha originly sprung
        from,
But having not had nothing to eat for some time, he
Was slepy and gap'd, in a short time, widely.
Unfoalding soon a welth of perl-white teth,
The rais of the son soon shet his sinister ey
Because of their mutool splendor and warmth.
The evil Our (which I sed) was now come;
Evidently a good chans for a water-snaik
Of the large specie, which soon appeared
Into the horison, near the bank where reposed
Calmly in slepe the Alegaiter before spoken of.
About 60 feet was his Length (not the 'gaiter)
And he was aperiently a well-proportioned snaik.
When he was all ashore he glared upon
The iland with approval, but was soon
" Astonished with the view and lost to wonder "
        (from Wats)
(For jest then he began to see the Alegaiter)
Being a nateral enemy of his'n, he worked hisself
Into a fury, also a ni position.

Before the Alegaiter well could ope
His eye (in other words perceive his danger)
The Snaik had enveloped his body just 19
Times with " foalds voluminous and vast " (from
    Milton)
And had tore off several scails in the confusion,
Besides squeazing him awfully into his stomoc.
Just then, by a fortinate turn in his affairs,
He ceazed into his mouth the careless tale
Of the unreflecting water-snaik ! Grown desperate
He, finding that his tale was fast squesed
Terrible while they roaled all over the iland.

It was a well-conduckted Affair ; no noise
Disturbed the harmony of the seen, ecsept
Onct when a Willow was snaped into by the roaling.
Eeach of the combatence had n't a minit for holering.
So the conflick was naterally tremenjous !
But soon by grate force the tail was bit complete-
Ly of ; but the eggzeration was too much
For his delicate Constitootion ; he felt a compres-
    sion
Onto his chest and generally over his body ;
When he ecspressed his breathing, it was with
Grate difficulty that he felt inspired again onct more.
Of course this state must suffer a revolootion.
So the alegaiter give but one yel, and egspired.
The water-snaik realed hisself off, & survay'd
For say 10 minits, the condition of
His fo : then wondering what made his tail hurt,
He slowly went off for to cool.

                                        J. W. Morris.

ODD TO A KROKIS

SELESTIAL apoley which Didest inspire.
the souls of burns and pop with sackred fir.
Kast thy Mantil over me When i shal sing.
the praiz Of A sweat flower who grows in spring.
Which has of late kome under the Fokis.
of My eyes.   It is called a krokis.
Sweat lovly prety littil sweat Thing.
you bloometh before The lairicks on High sing.
thy lefs are neithir Red Nor yelly.
but Just betwixt the two you hardy felly.

i fear youl yet be Nippit with the frost.
As Maney a one has known to there kost.
you should have not kome out in such a hurrey.
As this is only the Month of Febrywurrey.
and you may expick yet Much bad wethir.
when all your blads will krunkil up like Burnt
        leather.
alas.   alas.   theres Men which tries to rime.
who have like you kome out befor there time.
The Moril of My peese depend upon it.
is good so here i End my odd or sonit.

Anonymous.

SOME VERSES TO SNAIX

PRODIGGUS reptile! long and skaly kuss!
  You are the dadrattedest biggest thing I ever
  Seed that cud ty itself into a double bo-
Not, and cum all strate again in a
Minnit or so, without winkin or seemin
To experience any particular pane
In the diafram.

Stoopenjus inseck! marvelous annimile!
You are no doubt seven thousand yeres
Old, and hav a considerable of a
Family sneekin round thru the tall
Gras in Africa, a eetin up little greezy
Piggers, and wishin they was biggir.

I wonder how big yu was when yu
Was a inphant about 2 fete long.   I
Expec yu was a purty good size, and
Lived on phrogs, and lizzerds, and polly-
Wogs and sutch things.

You are havin' a nice time now, ennyhow —
Don't have nothing to do but lay oph.
And ete kats and rabbits, and stic
Out yure tung and twist yur tale.
I wunder if yu ever swollered a man
Without takin oph his butes.   If there was
Brass buttins on his kote, I spose

Yu had ter swaller a lot of buttin-
Wholes, and a shu-hamer to nock
The soals oph of the boots and drive in
The tax, so that they would n't kut yure
Inside.   I wunder if vittles taste
Good all the way down.   I expec so —
At leest, fur 6 or 7 fete.

You are so mighty long, I shud thynk
If your tale was kold, yure hed
Woodent no it till the next day,
But it 's hard tu tell : snaix is snaix.

Anonymous.

A GREAT MAN

YE muses, pour the pitying tear
    For Pollio snatch'd away :
      For had he liv'd another year !
—— He had not dy'd to-day.

O, were he born to bless mankind,
    In virtuous times of yore,
Heroes themselves had fallen behind !
    —— Whene'er he went before.

How sad the groves and plains appear,
    And sympathetic sheep :
Even pitying hills would drop a tear !
    —— If hills could learn to weep.

His bounty in exalted strain
 Each bard might well display :
Since none implor'd relief in vain !
 — That went reliev'd away.

And hark ! I hear the tuneful throng ;
 His obsequies forbid.
He still shall live, shall live as long
 — As ever dead man did.

     Oliver Goldsmith.

AN ELEGY

On the Glory of her Sex, Mrs. Mary Blaize

GOOD people all, with one accord,
 Lament for Madam Blaize,
 Who never wanted a good word —
From those who spoke her praise.

The needy seldom pass'd her door,
 And always found her kind ;
She freely lent to all the poor —
 Who left a pledge behind.

She strove the neighborhood to please
 With manners wondrous winning ;
And never follow'd wicked ways —
 Unless when she was sinning.

At church, in silks and satins new,
    With hoop of monstrous size,
She never slumber'd in her pew —
    But when she shut her eyes.

Her love was sought, I do aver,
    By twenty beaux and more;
The King himself has follow'd her —
    When she has walk'd before.

But now, her wealth and finery fled,
    Her hangers-on cut short all;
The doctors found, when she was dead —
    Her last disorder mortal.

Let us lament, in sorrow sore,
    For Kent Street well may say,
That had she lived a twelvemonth more —
    She had not died to-day.

                              Oliver Goldsmith.

PARSON GRAY

A QUIET home had Parson Gray,
        Secluded in a vale;
    His daughters all were feminine,
And all his sons were male.

How faithfully did Parson Gray
    The bread of life dispense —
Well " posted " in theology,
    And post and rail his fence.

'Gainst all the vices of the age
  He manfully did battle;
His chickens were a biped breed,
  And quadruped his cattle.

No clock more punctually went,
  He ne'er delayed a minute —
Nor ever empty was his purse,
  When he had money in it.

His piety was ne'er denied;
  His truths hit saint and sinner;
At morn he always breakfasted;
  He always dined at dinner.

He ne'er by any luck was grieved,
  By any care perplexed —
No filcher he, though when he preached,
  He always " took " a text.

As faithful characters he drew
  As mortal ever saw;
But ah! poor parson! when he died,
  His breath he could not draw!

Oliver Goldsmith.

AN ELEGY ON THE DEATH OF
A MAD DOG

GOOD people all, of every sort,
  Give ear unto my song;
  And if you find it wondrous short, —
It cannot hold you long.

In Islington there was a man,
   Of whom the world might say
'That still a godly race he ran, —
   Whene'er he went to pray.

A kind and gentle heart he had,
   To comfort friends and foes;
The naked every day he clad, —
   When he put on his clothes.

And in that town a dog was found,
   As many dogs there be,
Both mongrel, puppy, whelp, and hound,
   And curs of low degree.

The dog and man at first were friends;
   But when a pique began,
The dog, to gain some private ends,
   Went mad, and bit the man.

Around from all the neighboring streets,
   The wondering neighbors ran,
And swore the dog had lost his wits
   To bite so good a man.

The wound it seemed both sore and sad
   To every Christian eye;
And while they swore the dog was mad
   They swore the man would die.

But soon a wonder came to light,
   That showed the rogues they lied;
The man recovered of the bite,
   The dog it was that died.

               Oliver Goldsmith.

THE WONDERFUL OLD MAN

THERE was an old man
    Who lived on a common
    And, if fame speaks true,
He was born of a woman.
Perhaps you will laugh,
    But for truth I've been told
He once was an infant
    Tho' age made him old.

Whene'er he was hungry
    He longed for some meat;
And if he could get it
    'T was said he would eat.
When thirsty he'd drink
    If you gave him a pot,
And what he drank mostly
    Ran down his throat.

He seldom or never
    Could see without light,
And yet I've been told he
    Could hear in the night.

[153]

He has oft been awake
In the daytime, 't is said,
And has fallen asleep
As he lay in his bed.

'T is reported his tongue
Always moved when he talk'd,
And he stirred both his arms
And his legs when he walk'd;
And his gait was so odd
Had you seen him you 'd burst,
For one leg or t' other
Would always be first.

His face was the drollest
That ever was seen,
For if 't was not washed
It seldom was clean;
His teeth he expos'd when
He happened to grin,
And his mouth stood across
'Twixt his nose and his chin.

When this whimsical chap
Had a river to pass,
If he could n't get over
He stayed where he was.
'T is said he ne'er ventured
To quit the dry ground,
Yet so great was his luck
He never was drowned.

At last he fell sick,
 As old chronicles tell,
And then, as folks say,
 He was not very well.
But what was as strange
 In so weak a condition,
As he could not give fees
 He could get no physician.

What wonder he died!
 Yet 't is said that his death
Was occasioned at last
 By the loss of his breath.
But peace to his bones
 Which in ashes now moulder.
Had he lived a day longer
 He 'd have been a day older.

       Anonymous.

A CHRONICLE

ONCE — but no matter when —
 There lived — no matter where —
 A man, whose name — but then
I need not that declare.

He — well, he had been born,
 And so he was alive ;
His age — I details scorn —
 Was somethingty and five.

[155]

He lived — how many years
    I truly can't decide ;
But this one fact appears
    He lived — until he died.

" He died," I have averred,
    But cannot prove 't was so,
But that he was interred,
    At any rate, I know.

I fancy he 'd a son,
    I hear he had a wife :
Perhaps he 'd more than one,
    I know not, on my life !

But whether he was rich,
    Or whether he was poor,
Or neither — both — or which,
    I cannot say, I 'm sure.

I can't recall his name,
    Or what he used to do :
But then — well, such is fame !
    'T will so serve me and you.

And that is why I thus,
    About this unknown man
Would fain create a fuss,
    To rescue, if I can.

From dark oblivion's blow,
   Some record of his lot :
But, ah ! I do not know
   Who — where — when — why — or what.

MORAL

In this brief pedigree   .
   A moral we should find —
But what it ought to be
   Has quite escaped my mind !

Anonymous.

ON THE OXFORD CARRIER

HERE lieth one, who did most truly prove
     That he could never die while he could
       move ;
So hung his destiny never to rot
While he might still jog on and keep his trot ;
Made of sphere metal, never to decay
Until his revolution was at stay.
Time numbers motion, yet (without a crime
'Gainst old truth) motion number'd out his time,
And like an engine moved with wheel and weight,
His principles being ceased, he ended straight.
Rest, that gives all men life, gave him his death,
And too much breathing put him out of breath ;
Nor were it contradiction to affirm,
Too long vacation hasten'd on his term.

[157]

Merely to drive the time away he sicken'd,
Fainted, and died, nor would with ale be quicken'd;
" Nay," quoth he, on his swooning bed outstretch'd,
" If I may n't carry, sure I 'll ne'er be fetch'd,
But vow, though the cross doctors all stood hearers,
For one carrier put down to make six bearers."
Ease was his chief disease; and to judge right,
He died for heaviness that his cart went light :
His leisure told him that his time was come,
And lack of load made his life burdensome.
That even to his last breath (there be that say 't),
As he were press'd to death, he cried, " More
    weight ; "
But, had his doings lasted as they were,
He had been an immortal carrier.
Obedient to the moon he spent his date
In course reciprocal, and had his fate
Link'd to the mutual flowing of the seas,
Yet (strange to think) his wane was his increase :
His letters are deliver'd all, and gone,
Only remains the superscription.

John Milton.

NEPHELIDIA

FROM the depth of the dreamy decline of the
    dawn through a notable nimbus of
    nebulous noonshine,
Pallid and pink as the palm of the flag-flower that
    flickers with fear of the flies as they float,

Are they looks of our lovers that lustrously lean
   from a marvel of mystic miraculous moonshine,
These that we feel in the blood of our blushes
   that thicken and threaten with sobs from
   the throat ?
Thicken and thrill as a theatre thronged at appeal
   of an actor's appalled agitation,
Fainter with fear of the fires of the future than
   pale with the promise of pride in the past ;
Flushed with the famishing fulness of fever that
   reddens with radiance of rathe recreation,
Gaunt as the ghastliest of glimpses that gleam
   through the gloom of the gloaming when
   ghosts go aghast ?
Nay, for the nick of the tick of the time is a trem-
   ulous touch on the temples of terror,
Strained as the sinews yet strenuous with strife of
   the dead who is dumb as the dust-heaps of
   death :
Surely no soul is it, sweet as the spasm of erotic
   emotional exquisite error,
Bathed in the balms of beatified bliss, beatific itself
   by beatitude's breath.
Surely no spirit or sense of a soul that was soft to
   the spirit and soul of our senses
Sweetens the stress of suspiring suspicion that sobs
   in the semblance and sound of a sigh ;
Only this oracle opens Olympian, in mystical
   moods and triangular tenses —
Life is the lust of a lamp for the light that is dark
   till the dawn of the day when we die.

Mild is the mirk and monotonous music of memory melodiously mute as it may be,
While the hope in the heart of a hero is bruised
by the breach of men's rapiers resigned to
the rod;
Made meek as a mother whose bosom-beats bound
with the bliss-bringing bulk of a balm-
breathing baby,
As they grope through the grave-yards of creeds,
under skies growing green at a groan for
the grimness of God.
Blank is the book of his bounty beholden of old
and its binding is blacker than bluer :
Out of blue into black is the scheme of the skies,
and their dews are the wine of the blood-
shed of things;
Till the darkling desire of delight shall be free
as a fawn that is freed from the fangs that
pursue her,
Till the heart-beats of hell shall be hushed by
a hymn from the hunt that has harried the
kernel of kings.

A. C. Swinburne,
in " The Heptalogia."

MARTIN LUTHER AT POTSDAM

WHAT lightning shall light it ? What thunder shall tell it ?
In the height of the height, in the depth
of the deep ?

Shall the sea-storm declare it, or paint it, or smell
it ?
Shall the price of a slave be its treasure to
keep ?
When the night has grown near with the gems on
her bosom,
When the white of mine eyes is the whiteness
of snow,
When the cabman — in liquor — drives a blue roan,
a kicker,
Into the land of the dear long ago.

Ah ! — Ah, again ! — You will come to me, fall
on me —
You are *so* heavy, and I am *so* flat.
And I ? I shall not be at home when you call on
me,
But stray down the wind like a gentleman's
hat :
I shall list to the stars when the music is purple,
Be drawn through a pipe, and exhaled into
rings;
Turn to sparks, and then straightway get stuck in
the gateway
That stands between speech and unspeakable
things.

As I mentioned before, by what light is it lighted ?
Oh ! Is it fourpence, or piebald, or gray ?
Is it a mayor that a mother has knighted,
Or is it a horse of the sun and the day ?

[11]

Is it a pony?   If so, who will change it?
   O golfer, be quiet, and mark where it scuds,
And think of its paces — of owners and races —
   Relinquish the links for the study of studs.

Not understood?   Take me hence!   Take me
      yonder!
   Take me away to the land of my rest —
There where the Ganges and other gees wander,
   And uncles and antelopes act for the best,
And all things are mixed and run into each other
   In a violet twilight of virtues and sins,
With the church-spires below you and no one to
      show you
   Where the curate leaves off and the pew-rent
      begins!

In the black night through the rank grass the
      snakes peer —
   The cobs and the cobras are partial to grass —
And a boy wanders out with a knowledge of
      Shakespeare
   That's not often found in a boy of his class,
And a girl wanders out without any knowledge,
   And a bird wanders out, and a cow wanders out,
Likewise one wether, and they wander together —
   There's a good deal of wandering lying about.

But it's all for the best; I've been told by my
      friends, Sir,
   That in verses I'd written the meaning was
      slight;

I 've tried with no meaning — to make 'em amends,
    Sir —
  And find that this kind 's still more easy to write.
The title has nothing to do with the verses,
    But think of the millions — the laborers who
In busy employment find deepest enjoyment,
    And yet, like my title, have nothing to do!

Barry Pain.

COMPANIONS

I KNOW not of what we ponder'd
    Or made pretence to talk,
  As, her hand within mine, we wander'd
Tow'rd the pool by the limetree walk,
While the dew fell in showers from the passion
    flowers
  And the blush-rose bent on her stalk.

I cannot recall her figure :
    Was it regal as Juno's own ?
Or only a trifle bigger
    Than the elves who surround the throne
Of the Faëry Queen, and are seen, I ween,
    By mortals in dreams alone ?

What her eyes were like, I know not :
    Perhaps they were blurred with tears ;
And perhaps in your skies there glow not

(On the contrary) clearer spheres.
No ! as to her eyes I am just as wise
    As you or the cat, my dears.

Her teeth, I presume, were " pearly " :
    But which was she, brunette or blonde ?
Her hair, was it quaintly curly,
    Or as straight as a beadle's wand ?
That I failed to remark ; — it was rather dark
    And shadowy round the pond.

Then the hand that reposed so snugly
    In mine — was it plump or spare ?
Was the countenance fair or ugly ?
    Nay, children, you have me there !
My eyes were p'raps blurr'd ; and besides, I 'd heard
    That it 's horribly rude to stare.

And I — was I brusque and surly ?
    Or oppressively bland and fond ?
Was I partial to rising early ?
    Or why did we twain abscond,
All breakfastless too, from the public view
    To prowl by a misty pond ?

What passed, what was felt or spoken —
    Whether anything passed at all —
And whether the heart was broken
    That beat under that sheltering shawl —
(If shawl she had on, which I doubt) — has gone.
    Yes, gone from me past recall.

Was I haply the lady's suitor?
  Or her uncle? I can't make out —
Ask your governess, dears, or tutor.
  For myself, I'm in hopeless doubt
As to why we were there, and who on earth we
    were,
  And what this is all about.

C. S. Calverley.

THE COCK AND THE BULL

YOU see this pebble-stone? It's a thing I
      bought
    Of a bit of a chit of a boy i' the mid o' the
      day —
I like to dock the smaller parts-o-speech,
As we curtail the already cur-tailed cur
(You catch the paronomasia, play 'po' words?)
Did, rather, i' the pre-Landseerian days.
Well, to my muttons. I purchased the concern,
And clapt it i' my poke, having given for same
By way o' chop, swop, barter or exchange —
"Chop" was my snickering dandiprat's own term —
One shilling and fourpence, current coin o' the
    realm.
O-n-e one and f-o-u-r four
Pence, one and fourpence — you are with me,
    sir? —

What hour it skills not : ten or eleven o' the clock,
One day (and what a roaring day it was
Go shop or sight-see — bar a spit o' rain !)
In February, eighteen sixty nine,
Alexandrina Victoria, Fidei,
Hm — hm — how runs the jargon ? being on the
    throne.

Such, sir, are all the facts, succinctly put,
The basis or substratum — what you will —
Of the impending eighty thousand lines.
" Not much in 'em either," quoth perhaps simple
    Hodge.
But there 's a superstructure.   Wait a bit.

Mark first the rationale of the thing :
Hear logic rivel and levigate the deed.
That shilling — and for matter o' that, the pence —
I had o' course upo' me — wi' me say —
(*Mecum* 's the Latin, make a note o' that)
When I popp'd pen i' stand, scratched ear, wiped
    snout,
(Let everybody wipe his own himself)
Sniff'd — tch ! — at snuffbox; tumbled up, he-heed,
Haw-haw'd (not he-haw'd, that 's another guess
    thing) :
Then fumbled at, and stumbled out of, door,
I shoved the timber ope wi' my omoplat ;
And *in vestibulo*, i' the lobby to-wit,
(Iacobi Facciolati's rendering, sir,)
Donned galligaskins, antigropeloes,

And so forth; and, complete with hat and gloves,
One on and one a-dangle i' my hand,
And ombrifuge (Lord love you!) cas o' rain,
I flopped forth, 'sbuddikins! on my own ten toes,
(I do assure you there be ten of them)
And went clump-clumping up hill and down dale
To find myself o' the sudden i' front o' the boy.
Put case I had n't 'em on me, could I ha' bought
This sort-o'-kind-o'-what-you-might-call-toy,
This pebble-thing, o' the boy-thing? Q. E. D.
That 's proven without aid for mumping Pope,
Sleek porporate or bloated cardinal.
(Is n't it, old Fatchops? You 're in Euclid now.)
So, having the shilling — having i' fact a lot —
And pence and halfpence, ever so many o' them,
I purchased, as I think I said before,
The pebble (*lapis, lapidis, di, dem, de* —
What nouns 'crease short i' the genitive, Fat-
      chops, eh?)
O the boy, a bare-legg'd beggarly son of a gun,
For one-and-fourpence. Here we are again.
Now Law steps in, biwigged, voluminous-jaw'd;
Investigates and re-investigates.
Was the transaction illegal? Law shakes head.
Perpend, sir, all the bearings of the case.

At first the coin was mine, the chattel his.
But now (by virtue of the said exchange
And barter) *vice versa* all the coin,
Rer juris operationem, vests
I' the boy and his assigns till ding o' doom;

In sæcula sæculo-o-o-orum ;
(I think I hear the Abate mouth out that.)
To have and hold the same to him and them . . .
Confer some idiot on Conveyancing.
Whereas the pebble and every part thereof,
And all that appertaineth thereunto,
Quodcunque pertinet ad em rem,
(I fancy, sir, my Latin 's rather pat)
Or shall, will, may, might, can, could, would, or
    should,
Subaudi cætera — clap we to the close —
For what 's the good of law in such a case o' the
    kind
Is mine to all intents and purposes.
This settled, I resume the thread o' the tale.

Now for a touch o' the vendor's quality.
He says a gen'lman bought a pebble of him,
(This pebble i' sooth, sir, which I hold i' my
    hand) —
And paid for 't, *like* a gen'lman, on the nail.
" Did I o'ercharge him a ha'penny ?   Devil a bit.
Fiddlepin's end !   Get out, you blazing ass !
Gabble o' the goose.   Don't bugaboo-baby *me !*
Go double or quits ?   Yah ! tittup ! what 's the
    odds ? "
— There 's the transaction viewed in the vendor's
    light.

Next ask that dumpled hag, stood snuffling by,
With her three frowsy blowsy brats o' babes,

The scum o' the Kennel, cream o' the filth-heap —
    Faugh !
Aie, aie, aie, aie ! ὀτοτοτοτοτοῖ,
('Stead which we blurt out, Hoighty toighty now) —
And the baker and candlestick maker, and Jack
    and Gill,
Blear'd Goody this and queasy Gaffer that,
Ask the Schoolmaster, Take Schoolmaster first.
He saw a gentleman purchase of a lad
A stone, and pay for it *rite* on the square,
And carry it off *per saltum*, jauntily
Propria quæ maribus, gentleman's property now
(Agreeable to the law explained above).
In proprium usum, for his private ends,
The boy he chucked a brown i' the air, and bit
I' the face the shilling ; heaved a thumping stone
At a lean hen that ran cluck-clucking by,
(And hit her, dead as nail i' post o' door,)
Then *abiit* — What 's the Ciceronian phrase ?
Excessit, evasit, erupit — off slogs boy ;
Off like bird, *avi similis* — (you observed
The dative ? Pretty i' the Mantuan !) — *Anglice*
Off in three flea skips. *Hactenus*, so far,
So good, *tam bene*. *Bene, satis, male*, —
Where was I with my trope 'bout one in a quag ?
I did once hitch the Syntax into verse
Verbum personale, a verb personal,
Concordat — ay, " agrees," old Fatchops — *cum*
Nominativo, with its nominative,
Genere, i' point of gender, *numero*,
O' number, *et persona*, and person. *Ut*,
Instance : *Sol ruit*, down flops sun, *et* and,

Montes umbrantur, out flounce mountains.   Pah !
Excuse me, sir, I think I 'm going mad.

You see the trick on 't, though, and can yourself
Continue the discourse *ad libitum*.
It takes up about eighty thousand lines,
A thing imagination boggles at ;
And might, odds-bobs, sir ! in judicious hands
Extend from here to Mesopotamy.

C. S. Calverley.

LOVERS AND A REFLECTION

IN moss-prankt dells which the sunbeams flatter
    (And heaven it knoweth what that may
        mean ;
Meaning, however, is no great matter)
    Where woods are a-tremble with words a-tween ;

Thro' God's own heather we wonned together,
    I and my Willie (O love my love) :
I need hardly remark it was glorious weather,
    And flitter-bats wavered alow, above :

Boats were curtseying, rising, bowing,
    (Boats in that climate are so polite,)
And sands were a ribbon of green endowing,
    And O the sun-dazzle on bark and bight !

[170]

Thro' the rare red heather we danced together
   (O love my Willie,) and smelt for flowers :
I must mention again it was glorious weather,
   Rhymes are so scarce in this world of ours :

By rises that flushed with their purple favors,
   Thro' becks that brattled o'er grasses sheen,
We walked or waded, we two young shavers,
   Thanking our stars we were both so green.

We journeyed in parallels, I and Willie,
   In fortunate parallels ! Butterflies,
Hid in weltering shadows of daffodilly
   Or marjoram, kept making peacock eyes :

Song-birds darted about, some inky
   As coal, some snowy (I ween) as curds ;
Or rosy as pinks, or as roses pinky —
   They reek of no eerie To-come, those birds !

But they skim over bents which the mill-stream
      washes,
   Or hang in the lift 'neath a white cloud's hem ;
They need no parasols, no goloshes ;
   And good Mrs. Trimmer she feedeth them.

Then we thrid God's cowslips (as erst his heather),
   That endowed the wan grass with their golden
      blooms ;
And snapt— (it was perfectly charming weather) —
   Our fingers at Fate and her goddess-glooms :

And Willie 'gan sing — (Oh, his notes were
    fluty;
    Wafts fluttered them out to the white-winged
      sea) —
Something made up of rhymes that have done
      much duty,
    Rhymes (better to put it) of " ancientry " :

Bowers of flowers encountered showers
    In William's carol — (O love my Willie !)
Then he bade sorrow borrow from blithe to-
      morrow
    I quite forget what — say a daffodilly.

A nest in a hollow, " with buds to follow,"
    I think occurred next in his nimble strain ;
And clay that was " kneaden " of course in Eden —
    A rhyme most novel I do maintain :

Mists, bones, the singer himself, love-stories,
    And all least furlable things got furled ;
Not with any design to conceal their glories,
    But simply and solely to rhyme with world.

O if billows and pillows and hours and flowers,
    And all the brave rhymes of an elder day,
Could be furled together, this genial weather,
    And carted or carried on wafts away,
Nor ever again trotted out — ah me !
How much fewer volumes of verse there 'd be.

C. S. Calverley.

AN IMITATION OF WORDSWORTH

THERE is a river clear and fair,
　　'T is neither broad nor narrow;
　　It winds a little here and there —
It winds about like any hare;
And then it takes as straight a course
As on the turnpike road a horse,
　　Or through the air an arrow.

The trees that grow upon the shore,
Have grown a hundred years or more;
　　So long there is no knowing.
Old Daniel Dobson does not know
When first these trees began to grow;
But still they grew, and grew, and grew,
As if they 'd nothing else to do,
　　But ever to be growing.

The impulses of air and sky
Have rear'd their stately heads so high,
　　And clothed their boughs with green;
Their leaves the dews of evening quaff, —
　　And when the wind blows loud and keen,
I 've seen the jolly timbers laugh,
　　And shake their sides with merry glee —
　　Wagging their heads in mockery.

Fix'd are their feet in solid earth,
  Where winds can never blow;
But visitings of deeper birth
  Have reach'd their roots below.
For they have gain'd the river's brink,
And of the living waters drink.

There 's little Will, a five years child —
  He is my youngest boy:
To look on eyes so fair and wild,
  It is a very joy : —
He hath conversed with sun and shower,
And dwelt with every idle flower,
  As fresh and gay as them.
He loiters with the briar rose, —
The blue-belles are his play-fellows,
  That dance upon their slender stem.

And I have said, my little Will,
Why should not he continue still
  A thing of Nature's rearing?
A thing beyond the world's control —
A living vegetable soul, —
  No human sorrow fearing.

It were a blessed sight to see
That child become a Willow-tree,
  His brother trees among.
He 'd be four times as tall as me,
  And live three times as long.

Catharine M. Fanshawe.

THE FAMOUS BALLAD OF THE JUBILEE CUP

YOU may lift me up in your arms, lad, and
  turn my face to the sun,
 For a last look back at the dear old track
  where the Jubilee cup was won ;
And draw your chair to my side, lad — no, thank
 ye, I feel no pain —
For I 'm going out with the tide, lad ; but I 'll tell
 you the tale again.

I 'm seventy-nine or nearly, and my head it has
  long turned gray,
But it all comes back as clearly as though it was
 yesterday —
The dust, and the bookies shouting around the
 clerk of the scales,
And the clerk of the course, and the nobs in force,
 and 'Is 'Ighness the Pr**ce of W*les.

'T was a nine-hole thresh to wind'ard (but none of
 us cared for that),
With a straight run home to the service tee, and a
 finish along the flat,
"Stiff?" ah, well you may say it ! Spot barred, and
 at five stone ten !
But at two and a bisque I 'd ha' run the risk ; for
 I was a greenhorn then.

So we stripped to the B. Race signal, the old red
    swallowtail —
There was young Ben Bolt and the Portland Colt,
    and Aston Villa, and Yale;
And W. G., and Steinitz, Leander and The Saint,
And the G*rm*n Emp*r*r's Meteor, a-looking as
    fresh as paint;

John Roberts (scratch), and Safety Match, The
    Lascar, and Lorna Doone,
Oom Paul (a bye), and Romany Rye, and me upon
    Wooden Spoon;
And some of us cut for partners, and some of us
    strung for baulk,
And some of us tossed for stations — But there,
    what use to talk?

Three-quarter-back on the Kingsclere crack was
    station enough for me,
With a fresh jackyarder blowing and the Vicarage
    goal a-lee!
And I leaned and patted her centre-bit and eased
    the quid in her cheek,
With a " Soh my lass!" and a "Woa you brute!"
    — for she could do all but speak.

She was geared a thought too high perhaps; she
    was trained a trifle fine;
But she had the grand reach forward! I never saw
    such a line!

Smooth-bored, clean run, from her fiddle head with
its dainty ear half-cock,
Hard-bit, *pur sang*, from her overhang to the heel
of her off hind sock.

Sir Robert he walked beside me as I worked her
down to the mark ;
" There 's money on this, my lad," said he, " and
most of 'em 's running dark ;
But ease the sheet if you 're bunkered, and pack
the scrummages tight,
And use your slide at the distance, and we 'll drink
to your health to-night ! "

But I bent and tightened my stretcher.   Said I to
myself, said I —
" John Jones, this here is the Jubilee Cup, and
you have to do or die."
And the words were n't hardly spoken when the
umpire shouted " Play ! "
And we all kicked off from the Gasworks End with
a " Yoicks ! " and a " Gone Away ! "

And at first I thought of nothing, as the clay flew
by in lumps,
But stuck to the old Ruy Lopez, and wondered
who 'd call for trumps,
And luffed her close to the cushion, and watched
each one as it broke,
And in triple file up the Rowley Mile we went like
a trail of smoke.

[177]

The Lascar made the running but he did n't
    amount to much,
For old Oom Paul was quick on the ball, and
    headed it back to touch;
And the whole first flight led off with the right as
    The Saint took up the pace,
And drove it clean to the putting green and
    trumped it there with an ace.

John Roberts had given a miss in baulk, but Villa
    cleared with a punt;
And keeping her service hard and low the Meteor
    forged to the front;
With Romany Rye to windward at dormy and two
    to play,
And Yale close up — but a Jubilee Cup is n't run
    for every day.

We laid our course for the Warner — I tell you
    the pace was hot!
And again off Tattenham Corner a blanket covered
    the lot.
Check side! Check side! now steer her wide! and
    barely an inch of room,
With The Lascar's tail over our lee rail and brush-
    ing Leander's boom.

We were running as strong as ever — eight knots
    — but it could n't last;
For the spray and the bails were flying, the whole
    field tailing fast;

And the Portland Colt had shot his bolt, and Yale
    was bumped at the Doves,
And The Lascar resigned to Steinitz, stalemated in
    fifteen moves.

It was bellows to mend with Roberts — starred
    three for a penalty kick:
But he chalked his cue and gave 'em the butt, and
    Oom Paul marked the trick —
" Offside — No Ball — and at fourteen all! Mark
    Cock! and two for his nob!"
When W. G. ran clean through his lee and beat
    him twice with a lob.

He yorked him twice on a crumbling pitch and
    wiped his eye with a brace,
But his guy-rope split with the strain of it and he
    dropped back out of the race;
And I drew a bead on the Meteor's lead, and
    challenging none too soon,
Bent over and patted her garboard strake, and
    called upon Wooden Spoon.

She was all of a shiver forward, the spoondrift thick
    on her flanks,
But I'd brought her an easy gambit, and nursed
    her over the banks;
She answered her helm — the darling! and woke
    up now with a rush,
While the Meteor's jock, he sat like a rock — he
    knew we rode for his brush!

There was no one else left in it. The Saint was
    using his whip,
And Safety Match, with a lofting catch, was
    pocketed deep at slip;
And young Ben Bolt with his niblick took miss at
    Leander's lunge,
But topped the net with the ricochet, and Steinitz
    threw up the sponge.

But none of the lot could stop the rot — nay, don't
    ask *me* to stop!
The villa had called for lemons, Oom Paul had
    taken his drop,
And both were kicking the referee. Poor fellow!
    he done his best;
But, being in doubt, he'd ruled them out — which
    he always did when pressed.

So, inch by inch, I tightened the winch, and
    chucked the sandbags out —
I heard the nursery cannons pop, I heard the
    bookies shout:
" The Meteor wins!" "No, Wooden Spoon!"
    " Check!" "Vantage!" "Leg Before!"
" Last Lap!" "Pass Nap!" At his saddle-flap I
    put up the helm and wore.

You may overlap at the saddle-flap, and yet be
    loo'd on the tape:
And it all depends upon changing ends, how a
    seven-year-old will shape;

[180]

It was tack and tack to the Lepe and back — a fair
    ding-dong to the Ridge,
And he led by his forward canvas yet as we shot
    'neath Hammersmith Bridge.

He led by his forward canvas — he led from his
    strongest suit —
But along we went on a roaring scent, and at
    Fawley I gained a foot.
He fisted off with his jigger, and gave me his wash
    — too late !
Deuce — Vantage — Check ! By neck and neck
    we rounded into the straight.

I could hear the " Conquering 'Ero " a-crashing on
    Godfrey's band,
And my hopes fell sudden to zero, just there, with
    the race in hand —
In sight of the Turf's Blue Ribbon, in sight of the
    umpire's tape,
As I felt the tack of her spinnaker c-rack ! as I
    heard the steam escape !

Had I lost at that awful juncture my presence of
    mind ? . . . but no !
I leaned and felt for the puncture, and plugged it
    there with my toe . . .
Hand over hand by the Members' Stand I lifted
    and eased her up,
Shot — clean and fair — to the crossbar there, and
    landed the Jubilee Cup!

[181]

"The odd by a head, and leg before," so the Judge
    he gave the word :
And the umpire shouted "Over!" but I neither
    spoke nor stirred.
They crowded round : for there on the ground I
    lay in a dead-cold swoon,
Pitched neck and crop on the turf atop of my
    beautiful Wooden Spoon.

Her dewlap tire was punctured, her bearings all red
    hot;
She'd a lolling tongue, and her bowsprit sprung,
    and her running gear in a knot;
And amid the sobs of her backers, Sir Robert
    loosened her girth
And led her away to the knacker's. She had raced
    her last on earth!

But I mind me well of the tear that fell from the
    eye of our noble Pr*nce,
And the things he said as he tucked me in bed —
    and I've lain there ever since;
Tho' it all gets mixed up queerly that happened
    before my spill, —
But I draw my thousand yearly : it'll pay for the
    doctor's bill.

I'm going out with the tide, lad — you'll dig me
    a numble grave,
And whiles you will bring your bride, lad, and your
    sons, if sons you have,

And there when the dews are weeping, and the
    echoes murmur " Peace! "
And the salt, salt tide comes creeping and covers
    the popping-crease;

In the hour when the ducks deposit their eggs with
    a boasted force,
They 'll look and whisper " How was it? " and
    you 'll take them over the course,
And your voice will break as you try to speak of
    the glorious first of June,
When the Jubilee Cup, with John Jones up, was
    won upon Wooden Spoon.

Arthur T. Quiller-Couch.

A SONG OF IMPOSSIBILITIES

LADY, I loved you all last year,
    How honestly and well—
    Alas! would weary you to hear,
And torture me to tell;
I raved beneath the midnight sky,
    I sang beneath the limes—
Orlando in my lunacy,
    And Petrarch in my rhymes.
But all is over! When the sun
    Dries up the boundless main,
When black is white, false-hearted one,
    I may be yours again!

When passion's early hopes and fears
   Are not derided things;
When truth is found in falling tears,
   Or faith in golden rings;
When the dark Fates that rule our way
   Instruct me where they hide
One woman that would ne'er betray,
   One friend that never lied;
When summer shines without a cloud,
   And bliss without a pain;
When worth is noticed in a crowd,
   I may be yours again!

When science pours the light of day
   Upon the lords of lands;
When Huskisson is heard to say
   That Lethbridge understands;
When wrinkles work their way in youth,
   Or Eldon's in a hurry;
When lawyers represent the truth,
   Or Mr. Sumner Surrey;
When aldermen taste eloquence
   Or bricklayers champagne;
When common law is common sense,
   I may be yours again!

When learned judges play the beau,
   Or learned pigs the tabor;
When traveller Bankes beats Cicero,
   Or Mr. Bishop Weber;
When sinking funds discharge a debt,
   Or female hands a bomb;

When bankrupts study the *Gazette*,
   Or colleges *Tom Thumb*;
When little fishes learn to speak,
   Or poets not to feign;
When Dr. Geldart construes Greek,
   I may be yours again!

When Pole and Thornton honor cheques,
   Or Mr. Const a rogue;
When Jericho 's in Middlesex,
   Or minuets in vogue;
When Highgate goes to Devonport,
   Or fashion to Guildhall;
When argument is heard at Court,
   Or Mr. Wynn at all;
When Sydney Smith forgets to jest,
   Or farmers to complain;
When kings that are are not the best,
   I may be yours again!

When peers from telling money shrink,
   Or monks from telling lies;
When hydrogen begins to sink,
   Or Grecian scrip to rise;
When German poets cease to dream,
   Americans to guess;
When Freedom sheds her holy beam
   On Negroes, and the Press;
When there is any fear of Rome,
   Or any hope of Spain;
When Ireland is a happy home,
   I may be yours again!

When you can cancel what has been,
  Or alter what must be,
Or bring once more that vanished scene,
  Those withered joys to me ;
When you can tune the broken lute,
  Or deck the blighted wreath,
Or rear the garden's richest fruit,
  Upon a blasted heath ;
When you can lure the wolf at bay
  Back to his shattered chain,
To-day may then be yesterday —
  I may be yours again !

W. M. Praed.

TRUST IN WOMEN

When these things following be done to our intent,
Then put women in trust and confident.

WHEN nettles in winter bring forth roses
        red,
      And all manner of thorn trees bear figs
        naturally,
And geese bear pearls in every mead,
  And laurel bear cherries abundantly,
  And oaks bear dates very plenteously,
And kisks give of honey superfluence,
Then put women in trust and confidence.

When box bear paper in every land and town,
   And thistles bear berries in every place,
And pikes have naturally feathers in their crown,
   And bulls of the sea sing a good bass,
   And men be the ships fishes trace,
And in women be found no insipience,
Then put them in trust and confidence.

When whitings do walk forests to chase harts,
   And herrings their horns in forests boldly blow,
And marmsets mourn in moors and lakes,
   And gurnards shoot rooks out of a crossbow,
   And goslings hunt the wolf to overthrow,
And sprats bear spears in armès of defence,
Then put women in trust and confidence.

When swine be cunning in all points of music,
   And asses be doctors of every science,
And cats do heal men by practising of physic,
   And buzzards to scripture give any credence,
   And merchants buy with horn, instead of groats
      and pence,
And pyes be made poets for their eloquence,
Then put women in trust and confidence.

When sparrows build churches on a height,
   And wrens carry sacks unto the mill,
And curlews carry timber houses to dight,
   And fomalls bear butter to market to sell,
   And woodcocks bear woodknives cranes to kill,
And greenfinches to goslings do obedience,
Then put women in trust and confidence.

When crows take salmon in woods and parks,
　　And be take with swifts and snails,
And camels in the air take swallows and larks,
　　And mice move mountains by wagging of their
　　　　tails,
　　And shipmen take a ride instead of sails,
And when wives to their husbands do no offence,
Then put women in trust and confidence.

When antelopes surmount eagles in flight,
　　And swans be swifter than hawks of the tower,
And wrens set gos-hawks by force and might,
　　And muskets make verjuice of crabbes sour,
　　And ships sail on dry land, silt give flower,
And　apes　in　Westminster　give　judgment　and
　　　　sentence,
Then put women in trust and confidence.

Anonymous.

HERE IS THE TALE

AFTER RUDYARD KIPLING

Here is the tale — and you must make the most of it!
Here is the rhyme — ah, listen and attend!
Backwards — forwards — read it all and boast of it
If you are anything the wiser at the end!

NOW Jack looked up — it was time to sup,
　　　　and the bucket was yet to fill,
　　And Jack looked round for a space and
　　　　frowned, then beckoned his sister Jill,

And twice he pulled his sister's hair, and thrice he
    smote her side ;
" Ha' done, ha' done with your impudent fun —
    ha' done with your games ! " she cried ;
" You have made mud-pies of a marvellous size —
    finger and face are black,
You have trodden the Way of the Mire and Clay
    — now up and wash you, Jack !
Or else, or ever we reach our home, there waiteth
    an angry dame —
Well you know the weight of her blow — the
    supperless open shame !
Wash, if you will, on yonder hill — wash, if you
    will, at the spring, —
Or keep your dirt, to your certain hurt, and an
    imminent walloping ! "

" You must wash — you must scrub — you must
    scrape ! " growled Jack, " you must traffic
    with cans and pails,
Nor keep the spoil of the good brown soil in the
    rim of your finger-nails !
The morning path you must tread to your bath —
    you must wash ere the night descends,
And all for the cause of conventional laws and the
    soapmakers' dividends !
But if 't is sooth that our meal in truth depends on
    our washing, Jill,
By the sacred right of our appetite — haste — haste
    to the top of the hill ! "

They have trodden the Way of the Mire and Clay,
    they have toiled and travelled far,
They have climbed to the brow of the hill-top now,
    where the bubbling fountains are,
They have taken the bucket and filled it up — yea,
    filled it up to the brim;
But Jack he sneered at his sister Jill, and Jill she
    jeered at him:
" What, blown already! " Jack cried out (and his
    was a biting mirth!)
" You boast indeed of your wonderful speed — but
    what is the boasting worth?
Now, if you can run as the antelope runs, and if
    you can turn like a hare,
Come, race me, Jill, to the foot of the hill — and
    prove your boasting fair! "

" Race? What is a race " (and a mocking face had
    Jill as she spake the word)
" Unless for a prize the runner tries? The truth
    indeed ye heard,
For I can run as the antelope runs, and I can turn
    like a hare: —
The first one down wins half-a-crown — and I will
    race you there! "
" Yea, if for the lesson that you will learn (the
    lesson of humbled pride)
The price you fix at two-and-six, it shall not be
    denied;
Come, take your stand at my right hand, for here
    is the mark we toe:

Now, are you ready, and are you steady ? Gird up
　　your petticoats ! Go ! ”

And Jill she ran like a winging bolt, a bolt from
　　the bow released,
But Jack like a stream of the lightning gleam, with
　　its pathway duly greased ;
He ran down hill in front of Jill like a summer-
　　lightning flash —
Till he suddenly tripped on a stone, or slipped, and
　　fell to the earth with a crash.
Then straight did rise on his wondering eyes the
　　constellations fair,
Arcturus and the Pleiades, the Greater and Lesser
　　Bear,
The swirling rain of a comet's train he saw, as he
　　swiftly fell —
And Jill came tumbling after him with a loud
　　triumphant yell :
“ You have won, you have won, the race is done !
　　And as for the wager laid —
You have fallen down with a broken crown — the
　　half-crown debt is paid ! ”

They have taken Jack to the room at the back
　　where the family medicines are,
And he lies in bed with a broken head in a halo of
　　vinegar ;
While, in that Jill had laughed her fill as her
　　brother fell to earth,
She had felt the sting of a walloping — she hath
　　paid the price of her mirth !

[191]

Here is the tale — and now you have the whole of it,
Here is the story — well and wisely planned,
Beauty — Duty — these make up the soul of it —
But, ah, my little readers, will you mark and under-
stand?

Anthony C. Deane.

THE AULD WIFE

THE auld wife sat at her ivied door,
    (*Butter and eggs and a pound of cheese*)
    A thing she had frequently done before;
And her spectacles lay on her aproned knees.

The piper he piped on the hill-top high,
    (*Butter and eggs and a pound of cheese*)
Till the cow said "I die" and the goose asked
    "Why;"
And the dog said nothing, but searched for fleas.

The farmer he strode through the square farmyard;
    (*Butter and eggs and a pound of cheese*)
His last brew of ale was a trifle hard,
    The connection of which with the plot one sees.

The farmer's daughter hath frank blue eyes,
    (*Butter and eggs and a pound of cheese*)
She hears the rooks caw in the windy skies,
    As she sits at her lattice and shells her peas.

The farmer's daughter hath ripe red lips;
  (*Butter and eggs and a pound of cheese*)
If you try to approach her, away she skips
  Over tables and chairs with apparent ease.

The farmer's daughter hath soft brown hair;
  (*Butter and eggs and a pound of cheese*)
And I met with a ballad, I can't say where,
  Which wholly consisted of lines like these.

She sat with her hands 'neath her dimpled cheeks,
  (*Butter and eggs and a pound of cheese*)
And spake not a word.   While a lady speaks
  There is hope, but she did n't even sneeze.

She sat with her hands 'neath her crimson cheeks;
  (*Butter and eggs and a pound of cheese*)
She gave up mending her father's breeks,
  And let the cat roll in her best chemise.

She sat with her hands 'neath her burning cheeks
  (*Butter and eggs and a pound of cheese*),
And gazed at the piper for thirteen weeks;
  Then she followed him out o'er the misty leas.

Her sheep followed her as their tails did them
  (*Butter and eggs and a pound of cheese*),
And this song is considered a perfect gem,
  And as to the meaning, it's what you please.

                                    Charles S. Calverley.

NOT I

SOME like drink
   In a pint pot,
    Some like to think,
Some not.

Strong Dutch cheese,
   Old Kentucky Rye,
Some like these ;
   Not I.

Some like Poe,
   And others like Scott ;
Some like Mrs. Stowe,
   Some not.

Some like to laugh,
   Some like to cry,
Some like to chaff ;
   Not I.

R. L. Stevenson.

MINNIE AND WINNIE

MINNIE and Winnie
   Slept in a shell.
   Sleep, little ladies !
And they slept well.

[194]

Pink was the shell within,
    Silver without;
Sounds of the great sea
    Wandered about.

Sleep little ladies!
    Wake not soon!
Echo on echo
    Dies to the moon.

Two bright stars
    Peep'd into the shell,
What are they dreaming of?
    Who can tell?

Started a green linnet
    Out of the croft;
Wake, little ladies,
    The sun is aloft!

Lord Tennyson.

THE MAYOR OF SCUTTLETON *

THE Mayor of Scuttleton burned his nose
    Trying to warm his copper toes;
    He lost his money and spoiled his will
By signing his name with an icicle quill;
He went bareheaded, and held his breath,
And frightened his grandame most to death;
He loaded a shovel and tried to shoot,
And killed the calf in the leg of his boot;

* From "Rhymes and Jingles," copyright, 1874, 1902, Charles
Scribner's Sons.

He melted a snowbird and formed the habit
Of dancing jigs with a sad Welsh rabbit;
He lived on taffy and taxed the town;
And read his newspaper upside down;
Then he sighed and hung his hat on a feather,
And bade the townspeople come together;
But the worst of it all was, nobody knew
What the Mayor of Scuttleton next would do.

Mary Mapes Dodge.

THE PURPLE COW *

I NEVER saw a Purple Cow,
   I never hope to see one;
   But I can tell you, anyhow,
I'd rather see than be one.

Gelett Burgess.

THE INVISIBLE BRIDGE *

I'D Never Dare to Walk across
   A Bridge I Could Not See;
   For Quite afraid of Falling off,
I fear that I Should Be!

Gelett Burgess.

* By permission of Gelett Burgess; from " The Burgess Nonsense
Book," copyright, 1901.

THE LAZY ROOF *

THE Roof it has a Lazy Time
    A-lying in the Sun;
      The Walls they have to Hold Him Up;
They do Not Have Much Fun!

Gelett Burgess.

MY FEET *

MY feet, they haul me Round the House,
    They Hoist me up the Stairs;
      I only have to Steer them and
They Ride me Everywheres.

Gelett Burgess.

THE HEN †

ALAS! my Child, where is the Pen
    That can do Justice to the Hen?
      Like Royalty, She goes her way,
Laying foundations every day,
Though not for Public Buildings, yet
For Custard, Cake and Omelette.

* By permission of Gelett Burgess; from "The Burgess Nonsense Book," copyright, 1901.

† By permission of Oliver Herford; from "More Animals," copyright, 1901.

Or if too Old for such a use
They have their Fling at some Abuse,
As when to Censure Plays Unfit
Upon the Stage they make a Hit,
Or at elections Seal the Fate
Of an Obnoxious Candidate.
No wonder, Child, we prize the Hen,
Whose Egg is Mightier than the Pen.

Oliver Herford.

THE COW *

THE Cow is too well known, I fear,
    To need an introduction here.
    If She should vanish from earth's face
It would be hard to fill her place;
For with the Cow would disappear
So much that every one holds Dear.
Oh, think of all the Boots and Shoes,
Milk Punches, Gladstone Bags and Stews,
And Things too numerous to count,
Of which, my child, she is the Fount.
Let 's hope, at least, the Fount may last
Until *our* Generation 's past.

Oliver Herford.

* By permission of Oliver Herford ; from " More Animals," copyright, 1901.

THE CHIMPANZEE*

CHILDREN, behold the Chimpanzee :
 He sits on the ancestral tree
 From which we sprang in ages gone.
I 'm glad we sprang : had we held on,
We might, for aught that I can say,
Be horrid Chimpanzees to-day.

Oliver Herford.

THE HIPPOPOTAMUS*

OH, say, what is this fearful, wild,
 Incorrigible cuss ? ''
 " This *creature* (don't say ' cuss,' my child ;
'T is slang) — this creature fierce is styled
The Hippopotamus.
His curious name derives its source
From two Greek words : *hippos* — a horse,
Potamos — river. See ?
The river 's plain enough, of course ;
But why they called *that* thing a *horse*,
That 's what is Greek to me.''

Oliver Herford.

THE PLATYPUS*

MY child, the Duck-billed Platypus
 A sad example sets for us :
 From him we learn how Indecision
Of character provokes Derision.

* By permission of Oliver Herford ; from " A Child's Primer of
Natural History," copyright, 1899.

This vacillating Thing, you see,
Could not decide which he would be,
Fish, Flesh or Fowl, and chose all three.
The scientists were sorely vexed
To classify him; so perplexed
Their brains, that they, with Rage at bay,
Called him a horrid name one day, —
A name that baffles, frights and shocks us,
Ornithorhynchus Paradoxus.

Oliver Herford.

SOME GEESE *

EV-ER-Y child who has the use
Of his sen-ses knows a goose.
See them un-der-neath the tree
Gath-er round the goose-girl's knee,
While she reads them by the hour
From the works of Scho-pen-hau-er.

How pa-tient-ly the geese at-tend!
But do they re-al-ly com-pre-hend
What Scho-pen-hau-er's driv-ing at?
Oh, not at all; but what of that?
Nei-ther do I; nei-ther does she;
And, for that mat-ter, nor does he.

Oliver Herford.

* By permission of Oliver Herford; from "A Child's Primer of
Natural History," copyright, 1899.

THE FLAMINGO *

*Inspired by reading a chorus of spirits
in a German play*

FIRST VOICE.

OH! tell me have you ever seen a red, long-
        leg'd Flamingo?
    Oh! tell me have you ever yet seen him the
        water in go?

SECOND VOICE.

Oh! yes at Bowling-Green I 've seen a red long-
        leg'd Flamingo,
Oh! yes at Bowling-Green I 've there seen him
    the water in go.

FIRST VOICE.

Oh! tell me did you ever see a bird so funny
    stand-o
When forth he from the water comes and gets upon
    the land-o ?

SECOND VOICE.

No! in my life I ne'er did see a bird so funny
    stand-o
When forth he from the water comes and gets upon
    the land-o.

* By permission of D. Appleton & Co.

[201]

FIRST VOICE.

He has a leg some three feet long, or near it, so
they say, Sir.
Stiff upon one alone he stands, t' other he stows
away, Sir.

SECOND VOICE.

And what an ugly head he's got! I wonder that
he'd wear it.
But rather *more* I wonder that his long, thin neck
can bear it.

FIRST VOICE.

And think, this length of neck and legs (no doubt
they have their uses)
Are members of a little frame, much smaller than
a goose's!

BOTH.

Oh! isn't he a curious bird, that red, long-leg'd
Flamingo?
A water bird, a gawky bird, a sing'lar bird, by
jingo!

Lewis Gaylord Clark.

KINDNESS TO ANIMALS

SPEAK gently to the herring and kindly to the
    calf,
    Be blithesome with the bunny, at barnacles
      don't laugh !
Give nuts unto the monkey, and buns unto the bear,
Ne'er hint at currant jelly if you chance to see a
    hare !
Oh, little girls, pray hide your combs when tortoises
    draw nigh,
And never in the hearing of a pigeon whisper Pie !
But give the stranded jelly-fish a shove into the sea, —
Be always kind to animals wherever you may be !

Oh, make not game of sparrows, nor faces at the
    ram,
And ne'er allude to mint sauce when calling on a
    lamb.
Don't beard the thoughtful oyster, don't dare the
    cod to crimp,
Don't cheat the pike, or ever try to pot the playful
    shrimp.
Tread lightly on the turning worm, don't bruise
    the butterfly,
Don't ridicule the wry-neck, nor sneer at salmon-
    fry ;
Oh, ne'er delight to make dogs fight, nor bantams
    disagree, —
Be always kind to animals wherever you may be !

Be lenient with lobsters, and ever kind to crabs,
And be not disrespectful to cuttle-fish or dabs ;
Chase not the Cochin-China, chaff not the ox obese,
And babble not of feather-beds in company with
    geese.
Be tender with the tadpole, and let the limpet thrive,
Be merciful to mussels, don't skin your eels alive ;
When talking to a turtle don't mention calipee —
Be always kind to animals wherever you may be.

J. Ashby-Sterry.

SAGE COUNSEL

THE lion is the beast to fight,
    He leaps along the plain,
      And if you run with all your might,
He runs with all his mane.
    I 'm glad I 'm not a Hottentot,
      But if I were, with outward cal-lum
        I 'd either faint upon the spot
        Or hie me up a leafy pal-lum.

The chamois is the beast to hunt ;
    He 's fleeter than the wind,
And when the chamois is in front,
    The hunter is behind.
      The Tyrolese make famous cheese
      And hunt the chamois o'er the chaz-zums ;
      I 'd choose the former if you please,
      For precipices give me spaz-zums.

The polar bear will make a rug
    Almost as white as snow ;
But if he gets you in his hug,
    He rarely lets you go.
        And Polar ice looks very nice,
        With all the colors of a pris-sum ;
        But, if you 'll follow my advice,
        Stay home and learn your catechissum.

A. T. Quiller-Couch.

OF BAITING THE LION *

REMEMBERING his taste for blood
    You 'd better bait him with a cow ;
    Persuade the brute to chew the cud
Her tail suspended from a bough ;
It thrills the lion through and through
    To hear the milky creature moo.

Having arranged this simple ruse,
    Yourself you climb a neighboring tree ;
See to it that the spot you choose
    Commands the coming tragedy ;
Take up a smallish Maxim gun,
    A search-light, whisky, and a bun.

It 's safer, too, to have your bike
    Standing immediately below,
In case your piece should fail to strike,
    Or deal an ineffective blow ;

* By permission of John Lane ; from "In Cap and Bells," copyright, 1899.

The Lion moves with perfect grace,
    But cannot go the scorcher's pace.

Keep open ear for subtle signs ;
    Thus, when the cow profusely moans,
That means to say, the Lion dines.
    The crunching sound, of course, is bones ;
Silence resumes her ancient reign —
    This shows the cow is out of pain.

But when a fat and torpid hum
    Escapes the eater's unctuous nose,
Turn up the light and let it come
    Full on his innocent repose ;
Then pour your shot between his eyes,
    And go on pouring till he dies.

Play, even so, discretion's part ;
    Descend with stealth ; bring on your gun ;
Then lay your hand above his heart
    To see if he is really done ;
Don't skin him till you know he 's dead
    Or you may perish in his stead !

Years hence, at home, when talk is tall,
    You 'll set the gun-room wide agape,
Describing how with just a small
    Pea-rifle, going after ape
You met a Lion unaware,
    And felled him flying through the air.

Owen Seaman.

THE FROG

BE kind and tender to the Frog,
   And do not call him names,
      As " Slimy-Skin," or " Polly-wog,"
Or likewise, " Uncle James,"
Or "Gape-a-grin," or "Toad-gone-wrong,"
   Or " Billy-Bandy-knees ; "
The Frog is justly sensitive
   To epithets like these.

No animal will more repay
   A treatment kind and fair,
At least, so lonely people say
Who keep a frog (and, by the way,
   They are extremely rare).

Hilaire Belloc.

THE YAK

AS a friend to the children commend me the yak,
   You will find it exactly the thing :
      It will carry and fetch, you can ride on its
         back,
Or lead it about with a string.

A Tartar who dwells on the plains of Thibet
   (A desolate region of snow)
Has for centuries made it a nursery pet,
   And surely the Tartar should know !

[207]

Then tell your papa where the Yak can be got,
  And if he is awfully rich,
He will buy you the creature — or else he will not,
  (I cannot be positive which).

Hilaire Belloc.

THE PYTHON

A PYTHON I should not advise, —
  It needs a doctor for its eyes,
    And has the measles yearly.

However, if you feel inclined
To get one (to improve your mind,
  And not from fashion merely),
Allow no music near its cage;
And when it flies into a rage
  Chastise it most severely.

I had an Aunt in Yucatan
Who bought a Python from a man
  And kept it for a pet.
She died because she never knew
These simple little rules and few ; —
  The snake is living yet.

Hilaire Belloc.

THE BISON

THE Bison is vain, and (I write it with pain)
  The Door-mat you see on his head
  Is not, as some learned professors maintain,
The opulent growth of a genius' brain;
  But is sewn on with needle and thread.

Hilaire Belloc.

THE PANTHER

BE kind to the panther! for when thou wert
      young,
  In thy country far over the sea,
'T was a panther ate up thy papa and mamma,
  And had several mouthfuls of thee!

Be kind to the badger! for who shall decide
  The depths of his badgerly soul?
And think of the tapir when flashes the lamp
  O'er the fast and the free-flowing bowl.

Be kind to the camel! nor let word of thine
  Ever put up his bactrian back;
And cherish the she-kangaroo with her bag,
  Nor venture to give her the sack.

Be kind to the ostrich! for how canst thou hope
  To have such a stomach as it?
And when the proud day of your bridal shall come,
  Do give the poor birdie a bit.

[14]   [209]

Be kind to the walrus ! nor ever forget
   To have it on Tuesday to tea ;
But butter the crumpets on only one side,
   Save such as are eaten by thee.

Be kind to the bison ! and let the jackal
   In the light of thy love have a share ;
And coax the ichneumon to grow a new tail,
   And have lots of larks in its lair.

Be kind to the bustard ! that genial bird,
   And humor its wishes and ways ;
And when the poor elephant suffers from bile,
   Then tenderly lace up his stays !

Anonymous.

THE MONKEY'S GLUE

WHEN the monkey in his madness
   Took the glue to mend his voice,
    'T was the crawfish showed his sadness
That the bluebird could rejoice.

Then the perspicacious parrot
   Sought to save the suicide
By administering carrot,
   But the monkey merely died.

So the crawfish and the parrot
   Sauntered slowly toward the sea,
While the bluebird stole the carrot
   And returned the glue to me.

Goldwin Goldsmith.

THERE WAS A FROG

THERE was a frog swum in the lake,
  The crab came crawling by:
  " Wilt thou," coth the frog, "be my make ? "
Coth the crab, " No, not I."
" My skin is sooth and dappled fine,
  I can leap far and nigh.
Thy shell is hard: so is not mine."
  Coth the crab, " No, not I."
" Tell me," then spake the crab, " therefore,
  Or else I thee defy :
Give me thy claw, I ask no more."
  Coth the frog, " That will I."
The crab bit off the frog's fore-feet ;
  The frog then he must die.
To woo a crab it is not meet :
  If any do, it is not I.

From Christ Church MS., I. 549.

THE BLOATED BIGGABOON

THE bloated Biggaboon
  Was so haughty, he would not repose
  In a house, or a hall, or *ces choses*,
But he slept his high sleep in his clothes —
  'Neath the moon.

The bloated Biggaboon
Pour'd contempt upon waistcoat and skirt,
Holding swallow-tails even as dirt —
So he puft'd himself out in his shirt,
Like a b'loon.

H. Cholmondeley-Pennell.

WILD FLOWERS *

OF what are you afraid, my child?" inquired
the kindly teacher.
"Oh, sir! the flowers, they are wild,"
replied the timid creature.

Peter Newell.

TIMID HORTENSE *

NOW, if the fish will only bite, we'll have some
royal fun."
"And do fish bite? The horrid things!
Indeed, I'll not catch one!"

Peter Newell.

HER POLKA DOTS *

SHE played upon her music-box a fancy air by
chance,
And straightway all her polka-dots began a
lively dance.

Peter Newell.

* By permission of Harper & Brothers; from "Pictures and
Rhymes," copyright, 1900.

HER DAIRY *

A MILKWEED, and a buttercup, and cow-
slip," said sweet Mary,
" Are growing in my garden-plot, and this
I call my dairy."

Peter Newell.

TURVEY TOP

'TWAS after a supper of Norfolk brawn
That into a doze I chanced to drop,
And thence awoke in the gray of dawn,
In the wonder-land of Turvey Top.

A land so strange I never had seen,
And could not choose but look and laugh —
A land where the small the great includes,
And the whole is less than the half!

A land where the circles were not lines
Round central points, as schoolmen show,
And the parallels met whenever they chose,
And went playing at touch-and-go!

There — except that every round was square
And save that all the squares were rounds —
No surface had limits anywhere,
So they never could beat the bounds.

* By permission of Harper & Brothers; from " Pictures and
Rhymes," copyright, 1900.

In their gardens, fruit before blossom came,
   And the trees diminished as they grew;
And you never went out to walk a mile,
   'T was the mile that walked to you.

The people there are not tall or short,
   Heavy or light, or stout or thin,
And their lives begin where they should leave off,
   Or leave off where they should begin.

There childhood, with naught of childish glee,
   Looks on the world with thoughtful brow;
'T is only the aged who laugh and crow,
   And cry, " We have done with it now ! "

A singular race ! what lives they spent !
   Got up before they went to bed !
And never a man said what he meant,
   Or a woman meant what she said.

They blended colours that will not blend,
   All hideous contrasts voted sweet;
In yellow and red their Quakers dress'd,
   And considered it rather neat.

They did n't believe in the wise and good,
   Said the best were worst, the wisest fools;
And 't was only to have their teachers taught
   That they founded national schools.

They read in "books that are no books,"
  Their classics — chess-boards neatly bound;
Those their greatest authors who never wrote,
  And their deepest the least profound.

Now, such were the folks of that wonder-land,
  A curious people, as you will own;
But are there none of the race abroad,
  Are no specimens elsewhere known?

Well, I think that he whose views of life
  Are crooked, wrong, perverse, and odd,
Who looks upon all with jaundiced eyes —
  Sees himself and believes it God,

Who sneers at the good, and makes the ill,
  Curses a world he cannot mend;
Who measures life by the rule of wrong
  And abuses its aim and end,

The man who stays when he ought to move,
  And only goes when he ought to stop —
Is strangely like the folk in my dream,
  And would flourish in Turvey Top.

                              Anonymous.

WHAT THE PRINCE OF I DREAMT

I DREAMT it! such a funny thing —
    And now it's taken wing;
  I s'pose no man before or since
  Dreamt such a funny thing?

It had a Dragon; with a tail;
  A tail both long and slim,
And ev'ry day he wagg'd at it —
  How good it was of him!

And so to him the tailest
  Of all three-tailed Bashaws,
Suggested that for reasons
  The waggling should pause;

And held his tail — which, parting,
  Reversed that Bashaw, which
Reversed that Dragon, who reversed
  Himself into a ditch.

. . . . . .

It had a monkey — in a trap —
  Suspended by the tail:
Oh! but that monkey look'd distress'd,
  And his countenance was pale.

And he had danced and dangled there;
  Till he grew very mad:
For his tail it was a handsome tail
  And the trap had pinched it — bad.

The trapper sat below, and grinn'd;
  His victim's wrath wax'd hot:
He bit his tail in two — and fell —
  And killed him on the spot.

. . . . . .

It had a pig — a stately pig;
   With curly tail and quaint :
And the Great Mogul had hold of that
   Till he was like to faint.

So twenty thousand Chinamen,
   With three tails each at least,
Came up to help the Great Mogul,
   And took him round the waist.

And so, the tail slipp'd through his hands;
   And so it came to pass,
That twenty thousand Chinamen
   Sat down upon the grass.

   .   .   .   .   .   .

It had a Khan — a Tartar Khan —
   With tail superb, I wis;
And that fell graceful down a back
   Which was considered his.

Wherefore all sorts of boys that were
   Accursed, swung by it ;
Till he grew savage in his mind
   And vex'd, above a bit :

And so he swept his tail, as one
   Awak'ning from a dream ;
And those abominable ones
   Flew off into the stream.

Likewise they bobbled up and down,
    Like many apples there;
Till they subsided — and became
    Amongst the things that were.

  .   .   .   .   .   .

And so it had a moral too,
    That would be bad to lose;
" Whoever takes a Tail in hand
    Should mind his p's and queues."

I dreamt it! — such a funny thing!
    And now it's taken wing;
I s'pose no man before or since
    Dreamt such a funny thing?
              H. Cholmondeley-Pennell.

THE DINKEY–BIRD *

IN an ocean, 'way out yonder
    (As all sapient people know),
  Is the land of Wonder-Wander,
    Whither children love to go;
It 's their playing, romping, swinging,
    That give great joy to me
While the Dinkey-Bird goes singing
    In the Amfalula-tree!

There the gum-drops grow like cherries,
    And taffy's thick as peas, —
Caramels you pick like berries
    When, and where, and how you please:

* From " Poems of Childhood," copyright, 1892, by Mary French Field; 1894 by Eugene Field.

Big red sugar-plums are clinging
　To the cliffs beside that sea
Where the Dinkey-Bird is singing
　In the Amfalula-tree.

So when children shout and scamper
　And make merry all the day,
When there's naught to put a damper
　To the ardor of their play;
When I hear their laughter ringing,
　Then I'm sure as sure can be
That the Dinkey-Bird is singing
　In the Amfalula-tree.

For the Dinkey-Bird's bravuras
　And staccatos are so sweet —
His roulades, appogiaturas,
　And robustos so complete,
That the youth of every nation —
　Be they near or far away —
Have especial delectation
　In that gladsome roundelay.

Their eyes grow bright and brighter,
　Their lungs begin to crow,
Their hearts get light and lighter,
　And their cheeks are all aglow;
For an echo cometh bringing
　The news to all and me.
That the Dinkey-Bird is singing
　In the Amfalula-tree.

I 'm sure you 'd like to go there
  To see your feathered friend —
And so many goodies grow there,
  You would like to comprehend!
Speed, little dreams, your winging
  To that land across the sea
Where the Dickey-Bird is singing
  In the Amfalula-Tree!

Eugene Field.

THE MAN IN THE MOON *

SAID the Raggedy Man on a hot afternoon,
  "My!
        Sakes!
            What a lot o' mistakes
Some little folks makes on the Man in the Moon!
But people that 's been up to see him like Me,
And calls on him frequent and intimutly,
Might drop a few hints that would interest you
        Clean!
            Through!
                If you wanted 'em to —
Some actual facts that might interest you!

" O the Man in the Moon has a crick in his back;
        Whee!
            Whimm!
                Ain't you sorry for him?
And a mole on his nose that is purple and black;

* By permission of the author; from " Rhymes of Childhood,"
copyright, 1890, 1898.

And his eyes are so weak that they water and run
If he dares to *dream* even he looks at the sun, —
So he jes' dreams of stars, as the doctors advise —
   My!
      Eyes!
        But is n't he wise —
To jes' dream of stars, as the doctors advise?

" And the Man in the Moon has a boil on his ear —
   Whee!
      Whing!
        What a singular thing!
I know! but these facts are authentic, my dear, —
There 's a boil on his ear; and a corn on his chin,—
He calls it a dimple, — but dimples stick in, —
Yet it might be a dimple turned over, you know!
   Whang!
      Ho!
        Why certainly so! —
It might be a dimple turned over, you know!

" And the Man in the Moon has a rheumatic knee,
   Gee!
      Whizz!
        What a pity that is!
And his toes have worked round where his heels
   ought to be.
So whenever he wants to go North he goes South,
And comes back with the porridge crumbs all round
   his mouth,

And he brushes them off with a Japanese fan,
    Whing!
        Whann!
            What a marvellous man!
What a very remarkably marvellous man!

" And the Man in the Moon," sighed the Raggedy
    Man,
      "Gits!
        So!
            Sullonesome, you know!
Up there by himself since creation began! —
That when I call on him and then come away,
He grabs me and holds me and begs me to stay, —
Till — well, if it was n't for *Jimmy-cum-Jim*,
    Dadd!
      Limb!
        I 'd go pardners with him!
Jes' jump my bob here and be pardners with him!"

                James Whitcomb Riley.

THE STORY OF THE WILD HUNTSMAN

THIS is the Wild Huntsman that shoots the
    hares;
    With the grass-green coat he always wears;
With game-bag, powder-horn and gun,
He 's going out to have some fun.
He finds it hard without a pair
Of spectacles, to shoot the hare.

[222]

He put his spectacles upon his nose, and said,
"Now I will shoot the hares and kill them
    dead."
The hare sits snug in leaves and grass,
And laughs to see the green man pass.
Now as the sun grew very hot,
And he a heavy gun had got,
He lay down underneath a tree
And went to sleep as you may see.
'And, while he slept like any top,
The little hare came, hop, hop, hop, —
Took gun and spectacles, and then
Softly on tiptoe went off again.
The green man wakes, and sees her place
The spectacles upon her face.
She pointed the gun at the hunter's heart,
Who jumped up at once with a start.
He cries, and screams, and runs away.
"Help me, good people, help! I pray."
At last he stumbled at the well,
Head over ears, and in he fell.
The hare stopped short, took aim, and hark!
Bang went the gun! — she missed her mark!
The poor man's wife was drinking up
Her coffee in her coffee-cup;
The gun shot cup and saucer through;
"Oh dear!" cried she, "what shall I do?'
Hiding close by the cottage there,
Was the hare's own child, the little hare.
When he heard the shot he quickly arose,
And while he stood upon his toes,
The coffee fell and burned his nose;

" Oh dear," he cried, " what burns me so ? "
And held up the spoon with his little toe.

Dr. Heinrich Hoffman.

THE STORY OF PYRAMID
THOTHMES

THOTHMES, who loved a pyramid,
 And dreamed of wonders that it hid,
 Took up again one afternoon,
His longest staff, his sandal shoon,
His evening meal, his pilgrim flask,
And set himself at length the task,
Scorning the smaller and the small,
To climb the highest one of all.

The sun was very hot indeed,
Yet Thothmes never slacked his speed
Until upon the topmost stone
He lightly sat him down alone
To make himself some pleasant cheer
And turned to take his flask of beer,
For he was weary and athirst.
Forth from the neck the stopper burst
And rudely waked the sleeping dead.
In terror guilty Thothmes fled
As rose majestic, wroth and slow,
The Pharaoh's Ka of long ago.
" Help ! help ! " he cried, " or I am lost !
Oh ! save me from old Pharaoh's ghost ! "

Till, uttering one fearful yell,
He stumbled at the base and fell
Where Anubis was at his side,
And, by the god of death, he died.

The wife of Thothmes learned his tale
First from the " Memphis Evening Mail,"
And called her son, and told their woe ;
" Alas ! " said she, " I told him so !
Oh, think upon these awful things
And mount not on the graves of kings !
A pyramid is strange to see,
Though only at its base you be."

Anonymous.

THE STORY OF CRUEL PSAMTEK

HERE is cruel Psamtek, see.
Such a wicked boy was he !
Chased the ibis round about,
Plucked its longest feathers out,
Stamped upon the sacred scarab
Like an unbelieving Arab,
Put the dog and cat to pain,
Making them to howl again.
Only think what he would do —
Tease the awful Apis too !
Basking by the sacred Nile
Lay the trusting crocodile ;
Cruel Psamtek crept around him,
Laughed to think how he had found him,

With his pincers seized his tail,
Made the holy one to wail;
Till a priest of Isis came,
Called the wicked boy by name,
Shut him in a pyramid,
Where his punishment was hid.
— But the crocodile the while
Bore the pincers up the Nile —
Here the scribe who taught him letters,
And respect for all his betters,
Gave him many a heavy task,
Horrid medicines from a flask,
While on bread and water, too,
Bitter penance must he do.

The Crocodile is blythe and gay,
With friends and family at play,
And cries, " O blessed Land of Nile,
Where sacred is the crocodile,
Where no ill deed unpunished goes,
And man himself rewards our foes ! "

Anonymous.

THE CUMBERBUNCE

I STROLLED beside the shining sea,
I was as lonely as could be ;
No one to cheer me in my walk
But stones and sand, which cannot talk —
Sand and stones and bits of shell,
Which never have a thing to tell.

* By permission of Life Publishing Co. ; from " Life," copyright.

But as I sauntered by the tide
I saw a something at my side,
A something green, and blue, and pink,
And brown, and purple, too, I think.
I would not say how large it was;
I would not venture that, because
It took me rather by surprise,
And I have not the best of eyes.

Should you compare it to a cat,
I'd say it was as large as that;
Or should you ask me if the thing
Was smaller than a sparrow's wing,
I should be apt to think you knew,
And simply answer, "Very true!"

Well, as I looked upon the thing,
It murmured, "Please, sir, can I sing?"
And then I knew its name at once —
It plainly was a Cumberbunce.

You are amazed that I could tell
The creature's name so quickly?   Well,
I knew it was not a paper-doll,
A pencil or a parasol,
A tennis-racket or a cheese,
And, as it was not one of these,
And I am not a perfect dunce —
It had to be a Cumberbunce!

With pleading voice and tearful eye
It seemed as though about to cry.
It looked so pitiful and sad
It made me feel extremely bad.
My heart was softened to the thing
That asked me if it, please, could sing.
Its little hand I longed to shake,
But, oh, it had no hand to take!
I bent and drew the creature near,
And whispered in its pale blue ear,
" What ! Sing, my Cumberbunce ? You can !
Sing on, sing loudly, little man ! "

The Cumberbunce, without ado,
Gazed sadly on the ocean blue,
And, lifting up its little head,
In tones of awful longing, said :

" Oh, I would sing of mackerel skies,
    And why the sea is wet,
Of jelly-fish and conger-eels,
    And things that I forget.
And I would hum a plaintive tune
    Of why the waves are hot
As water boiling on a stove,
    Excepting that they 're not !

" And I would sing of hooks and eyes,
    And why the sea is slant,
And gayly tips the little ships,
    Excepting that I can't !

I never sang a single song,
  I never hummed a note.
There is in me no melody,
  No music in my throat.

" So that is why I do not sing
Of sharks, or whales, or anything ! "

I looked in innocent surprise,
My wonder showing in my eyes.
" Then why, O, Cumberbunce," I cried,
" Did you come walking at my side
And ask me if you, please, might sing,
When you could not warble anything ? "

" I did not ask permission, sir,
I really did not, I aver.
You, sir, misunderstood me, quite.
I did not ask you if I *might*.
Had you correctly understood,
You 'd know I asked you if I *could*.
So, as I cannot sing a song,
Your answer, it is plain, was wrong.
The fact I could not sing I knew,
But wanted your opinion, too."

A voice came softly o'er the lea.
" Farewell ! my mate is calling me ! "

I saw the creature disappear,
Its voice, in parting, smote my ear —
" I thought all people understood
The difference 'twixt ' might ' and ' could ' ! "

Paul West.

THE AHKOND OF SWAT

WHO, or why, or which, or *what*,
   Is the Ahkond of Swat?

Is he tall or short, or dark or fair?
Does he sit on a stool or sofa or chair,   or Squat,
   The Ahkond of Swat?

Is he wise or foolish, young or old?
Does he drink his soup and his coffee cold,   or Hot,
   The Ahkond of Swat?

Does he sing or whistle, jabber or talk,
And when riding abroad does he gallop or walk,
     or Trot,
   The Ahkond of Swat?

Does he wear a turban, a fez or a hat?
Does he sleep on a mattress, a bed or a mat,
     or a Cot,
   The Ahkond of Swat?

When he writes a copy in round-hand size,
Does he cross his t's and finish his i's
     with a Dot,
   The Ahkond of Swat?

Can he write a letter concisely clear,
Without a speck or a smudge or smear   or Blot,
   The Ahkond of Swat?

Do his people like him extremely well ?
Or do they, whenever they can, rebel,   or Plot,
           At the Ahkond of Swat ?

If he catches them tnen, either old or young,
Does he have them chopped in pieces or hung,
                 or Shot,
           The Ahkond of Swat ?

Do his people prig in the lanes or park ?
Or even at times, when days are dark,   Garotte ?
           Oh, the Ahkond of Swat ?

Does he study the wants of his own dominion ?
Or does n't he care for public opinion   a Jot,
           The Ahkond of Swat ?

To amuse his mind do his people show him
Pictures, or any one's last new poem,   or What,
           For the Ahkond of Swat ?

At night if he suddenly screams and wakes,
Do they bring him only a few small cakes,
               or a Lot,
           For the Ahkond of Swat ?

Does he live on turnips, tea or tripe,
Does he like his shawl to be marked with a stripe
               or a Dot,
           The Ahkond of Swat ?

Does he like to lie on his back in a boat
Like the lady who lived in that isle remote,
                             Shalott.
            The Ahkond of Swat?

Is he quiet, or always making a fuss?
Is his steward a Swiss or a Swede or a Russ,
                       or a Scot,
            The Ahkond of Swat?

Does he like to sit by the calm blue wave?
Or to sleep and snore in a dark green cave,
                      or a Grott,
            The Ahkond of Swat?

Does he drink small beer from a silver jug?
Or a bowl? or a glass? or a cup? or a mug?
                      or a Pot,
            The Ahkond of Swat?

Does he beat his wife with a gold-topped pipe,
When she lets the gooseberries grow too ripe,
                      or a Rot,
            The Ahkond of Swat?

Does he wear a white tie when he dines with his
    friends,
And tie it neat in a bow with ends,   or a Knot,
            The Ahkond of Swat?

Does he like new cream, and hate mince-pies?
When he looks at the sun does he wink his eyes,
                                        or Not,
                    The Ahkond of Swat?

Does he teach his subjects to roast and bake?
Does he sail about on an inland lake,
                                        in a Yacht,
                    The Ahkond of Swat?

Some one, or nobody knows I wot
Who or which or why or what
                    Is the Ahkond of Swat!

Edward Lear.

A THRENODY

WHAT, what, what,
        What 's the news from Swat?
        Sad news,
        Bad news,
Comes by the cable led
Through the Indian Ocean's bed,
Through the Persian Gulf, the Red
Sea and the Med-
Iterranean — he 's dead;
The Ahkoond is dead!

For the Ahkoond I mourn,
    Who would n't?
He strove to disregard the mesage stern,
    But he Ahkood n't.
Dead, dead, dead ;
    (Sorrow Swats !)
Swats wha hae wi' Ahkoond bled,
Swats whom he hath often led
Onward to a gory bed,
    Or to Victory,
    As the case might be,
      Sorrow Swats !
Tears shed,
    Tears shed like water,
Your great Ahkoond is dead !
That Swats the matter !

Mourn, city of Swat !
Your great Ahkoond is not,
But lain 'mid worms to rot.
His mortal part alone, his soul was caught
    (Because he was a good Ahkoond)
    Up to the bosom of Mahound.
Though earthly walls his frame surround
(Forever hallowed be the ground !)
And sceptics mock the lowly mound
And say " He 's now of no Ahkoond ! "
    His soul is in the skies —
The azure skies that bend above his loved
    Metropolis of Swat.

He sees with larger, other eyes,
Athwart all earthly mysteries —
He knows what's Swat.

Let Swat bury the great Ahkoond
    With a noise of mourning and of lamentation!
Let Swat bury the great Ahkoond
    With the noise of the mourning of the Swattish
        nation!
        Fallen is at length
        Its tower of strength,
Its sun is dimmed ere it had nooned;
Dead lies the great Ahkoond,
        The great Ahkoond of Swat
        Is not!

George Thomas Lanigan.

DIRGE OF THE MOOLLA
OF KOTAL

Rival of the Akhoond of Swat

I

ALAS, unhappy land; ill-fated spot
    Kotal — though where or what
    On earth Kotal is, the bard has forgot;
Further than this indeed he knoweth not —
It borders upon Swat!

II

When sorrows come, they come not single spies,
　　But in battal-
Ions : the gloom that lay on Swat now lies
　　Upon Kotal,
On sad Kotal, whose people ululate
For their loved Mooila late.
Put away his little turban,
And his narghileh embrowned,
The lord of Kotal — rural urban —
'S gone unto his last Akhoond,
'S gone to meet his rival Swattan,
'S gone, indeed, but not forgotten.

III

His rival, but in what ?
Wherein did the deceased Akhoond of Swat
Kotal's lamented Moolla late,
As it were, emulate ?
Was it in the tented field
With crash of sword on shield,
While backward meaner champions reeled
And loud the tom-tom pealed ?
Did they barter gash for scar
With the Persian scimetar
Or the Afghanistee tulwar,
While loud the tom-tom pealed —
While loud the tom-tom pealed,
And the jim-jam squealed,
And champions less well heeled
Their war-horses wheeled

And fled the presence of these mortal big bugs o'
    the field?
Was Kotal's proud citadel —
Bastioned, and demi-luned,
Beaten down with shot and shell
By the guns of the Akhoond?
Or were wails despairing caught, as
The burghers pale of Swat
Cried in panic, " Moolla ad Portas " ?
    — Or what?
Or made each in the cabinet his mark
Kotalese Gortschakoff, Swattish Bismarck?
Did they explain and render hazier
The policies of Central Asia?
Did they with speeches from the throne,
    Wars dynastic,
Ententes cordiales,
Between Swat and Kotal;
Holy alliances,
And other appliances
Of statesmen with morals and consciences
    plastic
Come by much more than their own?
Made they mots, as " There to-day are
No more Himalayehs,"
Or, if you prefer it, " There to-day are
No more Himalaya " ?
Or, said the Akhoond, " Sah,
L'État de Swat c'est moi " ?
Khabu, did there come great fear
On thy Khabuldozed Ameer
    Ali Shere?

Or did the Khan of far
    Kashgar
Tremble at the menace hot
Of the Moolla of Kotal,
" I will extirpate thee, pal
Of my foe the Akhoond of Swat " ?
    Who knows
Of Moolla and Akhoond aught more than I did ?
Namely, in life they rivals were, or foes,
And in their deaths not very much divided ?
If any one knows it,
Let him disclose it !

George Thomas Lanigan.

RUSSIAN AND TURK

THERE was a Russian came over the sea,
    Just when the war was growing hot ;
    And his name it was Tjalikavakaree-
Karindobrolikanahudarot-
    Shibkadirova-
    Ivarditztova
    Sanilik
    Danerik
    Varagobhot.

A Turk was standing upon the shore-
    Right where the terrible Russian crossed,
And he cried : " Bismillah ! I 'm Ab-El Kor-
    Bazarou-Kilgonautosgobross-

Getfinpravadi-
Kligekoladji
Grivino
Blivido-
Jenikodosk!

So they stood like brave men long and well;
  And they called each other their proper names,
Till the lockjaw seized them, and where they fell
  They buried them both by the Irdesholmmes
    Kalatalustchuk
    Mischtaribusiclup-
    Bulgari-
    Dulbary-
    Sagharimsing.

Anonymous.

LINES TO MISS FLORENCE
HUNTINGDON

SWEET maiden of Passamaquoddy,
  Shall we seek for communion of souls
  Where the deep Mississippi meanders,
Or the distant Saskatchewan rolls?

Ah no, — for in Maine I will find thee
  A sweetly sequestrated nook,
Where the far-winding Skoodoowabskooksis
Conjoins with the Skoodoowabskook.

[239]

There wander two beautiful rivers,
  With many a winding and crook;
The one is the Skoodoowabskooksis,
  The other — the Skoodoowabskook.

Ah, sweetest of haunts! though unmentioned
  In geography, atlas, or book,
How fair is the Skoodoowabskooksis,
  When joining the Skoodoowabskook!

Our cot shall be close by the waters
  Within that sequestrated nook —
Reflected in Skoodoowabskooksis
  And mirrored in Skoodoowabskook.

You shall sleep to the music of leaflets,
  By zephyrs in wantonness shook,
And dream of the Skoodoowabskooksis,
  And, perhaps, of the Skoodoowabskook.

When awaked by the hens and the roosters,
  Each morn, you shall joyously look
On the junction of Skoodoowabskooksis
  With the soft gliding Skoodoowabskook.

Your food shall be fish from the waters,
  Drawn forth on the point of a hook,
From murmuring Skoodoowabskooksis,
  Or wandering Skoodoowabskook!

You shall quaff the most sparkling of water,
  Drawn forth from a silvery brook
Which flows to the Skoodoowabskooksis,
  And then to the Skoodoowabskook!

And you shall preside at the banquet,
  And I will wait on thee as cook;
And we'll talk of the Skoodoowabskooksis,
  And sing of the Skoodoowabskook!

Let others sing loudly of Saco,
  Of Quoddy, and Tattamagouche,
Of Kennebeccasis, and Quaco,
  Of Merigonishe, and Buctouche,

Of Nashwaak, and Magaguadavique,
  Or Memmerimammericook, —
There's none like the Skoodoowabskooksis,
  Excepting the Skoodoowabskook!

Anonymous.

COBBE'S PROPHECIES

WHEN the day and the night do meete
    And the houses are even with the streete:
    And the fire and the water agree,
And blinde men have power to see:
When the Wolf and the Lambe lie down togither,
And the blasted trees will not wither:
When the flood and the ebbe run one way,
And the Sunne and the Moone are at a stay;

When Age and Youth are all one,
And the Miller creepes through the Mill-stone :
When the Ram butts the Butcher on the head,
And the living are buried with the dead.
When the Cobler doth worke without his ends,
And the Cutpurse and the Hangman are friends :
Strange things will then be to see,
But I think it will never be !

— *1614.*

AN UNSUSPECTED FACT

IF down his throat a man should choose
In fun, to jump or slide,
He 'd scrape his shoes against his teeth,
Nor dirt his own inside.
But if his teeth were lost and gone,
And not a stump to scrape upon,
He 'd see at once how very pat
His tongue lay there by way of mat,
And he would wipe his feet on *that* !

Edward Cannon.

THE SORROWS OF WERTHER

WERTHER had a love for Charlotte
Such as words could never utter ;
Would you know how first he met her ?
She was cutting bread and butter.

Charlotte was a married lady,
    And a moral man was Werther,
And for all the wealth of Indies,
    Would do nothing for to hurt her.

So he sigh'd and pined and ogled,
    And his passion boil'd and bubbled,
Till he blew his silly brains out,
    And no more was by it troubled.

Charlotte, having seen his body
    Borne before her on a shutter,
Like a well-conducted person,
    Went on cutting bread and butter.

W. M. Thackeray.

NONSENSE VERSES

LAZY-BONES, lazy-bones, wake up and peep!
    The cat's in the cupboard, your mother's
        asleep.
There you sit snoring, forgetting her ills;
Who is to give her her Bolus and Pills?
Twenty fine Angels must come into town,
All for to help you to make your new gown:
Dainty aerial Spinsters and Singers;
Are n't you ashamed to employ such white fingers?
Delicate hands, unaccustom'd to reels,
To set 'em working a poor body's wheels?
Why they came down is to me all a riddle,
And left Hallelujah broke off in the middle:

Jove's Court, and the Presence angelical, cut —
To eke out the work of a lazy young slut.
Angel-duck, Angel-duck, winged and silly,
Pouring a watering-pot over a lily,
Gardener gratuitous, careless of pelf,
Leave her to water her lily herself,
Or to neglect it to death if she chuse it :
Remember the loss is her own if she lose it.

Charles Lamb.

THE NOBLE TUCK--MAN

AMERICUS, as he did wend
    With A. J. Mortimer, his chum,
    The two were greeted by a friend,
" And how are you, boys, Hi, Ho, Hum ? "

He spread a note so crisp, so neat
    (Ho, and Hi, and tender Hum),
" If you of this a fifth can eat
    I 'll give you the remainder. Come! "

To the tuck-shop three repair,
    (Ho, and Hum, and pensive Hi),
One looks on to see all 's fair,
    Two call out for hot mince-pie.

Thirteen tarts, a few Bath buns
    (Hi, and Hum, and gorgeous Ho),
Lobster cakes (the butter'd ones),
    All at once they cry, " No go."

Then doth tuck-man smile. "Them there
  (Ho, and Hi, and futile Hum)
Jellies three and sixpence air,
  Use of spoons an equal sum."

Three are rich. Sweet task 't is o'er,
  "Tuckman, you 're a brick," they cry,
Wildly then shake hands all four
  (Hum and Ho, the end is Hi).

Jean Ingelow.

THE PESSIMIST *

NOTHING to do but work,
  Nothing to eat but food,
  Nothing to wear but clothes
To keep one from going nude.

Nothing to breathe but air,
  Quick as a flash 't is gone;
Nowhere to fall but off,
  Nowhere to stand but on.

Nothing to comb but hair,
  Nowhere to sleep but in bed,
Nothing to weep but tears,
  Nothing to bury but dead.

* By permission of Forbes & Co. ; from "Ben King's Verses,"
copyright, 1894, 1898.

Nothing to sing but songs,
　　Ah, well, alas ! alack !
Nowhere to go but out,
　　Nowhere to come but back.

Nothing to see but sights,
　　Nothing to quench but thirst,
Nothing to have but what we 've got ;
　　Thus thro' life we are cursed.

Nothing to strike but a gait ;
　　Everything moves that goes.
Nothing at all but common sense
　　Can ever withstand these woes.

Ben King.

THE MODERN HIAWATHA

HE killed the noble Mudjokivis.
　　Of the skin he made him mittens,
　　Made them with the fur side inside,
Made them with the skin side outside.
He, to get the warm side inside,
Put the inside skin side outside ;
He, to get the cold side outside,
Put the warm side fur side inside.
That 's why he put the fur side inside,
Why he put the skin side outside,
Why he turned them inside outside.

Anonymous.

ON THE ROAD*

SAID Folly to Wisdom,
  " Pray, where are we going ? "
Said Wisdom to Folly,
  " There's no way of knowing."

Said Folly to Wisdom,
  " Then what shall we do ? "
Said Wisdom to Folly,
  " I thought to ask you."

Tudor Jenks.

UNCLE SIMON AND UNCLE JIM

UNCLE Simon he
    Clum up a tree
    To see what he could see
When presentlee
Uncle Jim
Clum up beside of him
And squatted down by he.

Artemus Ward.

POOR DEAR GRANDPAPA

WHAT is the matter with Grandpapa ?
    What can the matter be ?
    He's broken his leg in trying to spell
Tommy without a T.

D'Arcy W. Thompson.

* By permission of the author.

[247]

THE SEA–SERPENT

ALL bones but yours will rattle when I say
I 'm the sea-serpent from America.
Mayhap you 've heard that I 've been round
the world ;
I guess I 'm round it now, Mister, twice curled.
Of all the monsters through the deep that splash,
I 'm " number one " to all immortal smash.
When I lie down and would my length unroll,
There ar' n't half room enough 'twixt pole and
pole.
In short, I grow so long that I 've a notion
I must be measured soon for a new ocean.

Planché.

MELANCHOLIA

I AM a peevish student, I ;
My star is gone from yonder sky.
I think it went so high at first
That it just went and gone and burst.

Anonymous.

THE MONKEY'S WEDDING

THE monkey married the Baboon's sister,
Smacked his lips and then he kissed her,
He kissed so hard he raised a blister.
She set up a yell.

The bridesmaid stuck on some court plaster,
It stuck so fast it could n't stick faster,
Surely 't was a sad disaster,
    But it soon got well.

What do you think the bride was dressed in ?
White gauze veil and a green glass breast-pin,
Red kid shoes — she was quite interesting,
    She was quite a belle.
The bridegroom swell'd with a blue shirt collar,
Black silk stock that cost a dollar,
Large false whiskers the fashion to follow ;
    He cut a monstrous swell.

What do you think they had for supper ?
Black-eyed peas and bread and butter,
Ducks in the duck-house all in a flutter,
    Pickled oysters too.
Chestnuts raw and boil'd and roasted,
Apples sliced and onions toasted,
Music in the corner posted,
    Waiting for the cue.

What do you think was the tune they danced to ?
" The drunken Sailor " — sometimes " Jim Crow,"
Tails in the way — and some got pinched, too,
    'Cause they were too long.
What do you think they had for a fiddle ?
An old Banjo with a hole in the middle,
A Tambourine made out of a riddle,
    And that 's the end of my song.

                    Anonymous.

MR. FINNEY'S TURNIP

MR. FINNEY had a turnip
    And it grew and it grew;
    And it grew behind the barn,
And that turnip did no harm.

There it grew and it grew
    Till it could grow no longer;
Then his daughter Lizzie picked it
    And put it in the cellar.

There it lay and it lay
    Till it began to rot;
And his daughter Susie took it
    And put it in the pot.

And they boiled it and boiled it
    As long as they were able,
And then his daughters took it
    And put it on the table.

Mr. Finney and his wife
    They sat down to sup;
And they ate and they ate
    And they ate that turnip up.

Anonymous.

THE SUN

THE Sun, yon glorious orb of day,
　　Ninety-four million miles away,
　　Will keep revolving in its orbit
Till heat and motion reabsorb it.

J. Davis.

THE AUTUMN LEAVES

THE Autumn leaves are falling,
　　Are falling here and there.
　　They 're falling through the atmosphere
And also through the air.

Anonymous.

IN THE NIGHT

THE night was growing old
　　As she trudged through snow and sleet；
　　Her nose was long and cold,
And her shoes were full of feet.

Anonymous.

POOR BROTHER

HOW very sad it is to think
　　Our poor benighted brother
　　Should have his head upon one end,
His feet upon the other.

Anonymous.

[251]

THE BOY *

DOWN through the snow-drifts in the street
    With blustering joy he steers;
    His rubber boots are full of feet
And his tippet full of ears.

                       Eugene Field.

THE SEA

BEHOLD the wonders of the mighty deep,
    Where crabs and lobsters learn to creep,
    And little fishes learn to swim,
And clumsy sailors tumble in.

                       Anonymous.

THERE WAS A LITTLE GIRL

THERE was a little girl,
    And she had a little curl
        Right in the middle of her forehead.
When she was good
She was very, very good,
    And when she was bad she was horrid.

One day she went upstairs,
When her parents, unawares,
    In the kitchen were occupied with meals
And she stood upon her head
In her little trundle-bed,
    And then began hooraying with her heels.

* From " Sharps and Flats," copyright, 1900, by Julia Sutherland Field.

[252]

Her mother heard the noise,
And she thought it was the boys
   A-playing at a combat in the attic;
But when she climbed the stair,
And found Jemima there,
   She took and she did spank her most emphatic.

H. W. Longfellow.

FIN DE SIÈCLE

THE sorry world is sighing now;
   La Grippe is at the door;
   And many folks are dying now
Who never died before.

Newton Mackintosh.

MARY JANE

MARY JANE was a farmer's daughter,
   Mary Jane did what she oughter.
   She fell in love — but all in vain;
Oh, poor Mary! oh, poor Jane!

Anonymous.

TENDER–HEARTEDNESS *

LITTLE Willie, in the best of sashes,
   Fell in the fire and was burned to ashes.
   By and by the room grew chilly,
But no one liked to poke up Willie.

Col. D. Streamer.

---

* By permission of R. H. Russell; from " Ruthless Rhymes for
Heartless Homes," copyright, 1901.

[253]

IMPETUOUS SAMUEL *

SAM had spirits naught could check,
  And to-day, at breakfast, he
  Broke his baby sister's neck,
So he sha'n't have jam for tea !

Col. D. Streamer.

MISFORTUNES NEVER COME SINGLY *

MAKING toast at the fireside,
  Nurse fell in the grate and died;
  And, what makes it ten times worse,
All the toast was burned with Nurse.

Col. D. Streamer.

AUNT ELIZA *

IN the drinking-well
  (Which the plumber built her)
  Aunt Eliza fell, —
We must buy a filter.

Col. D. Streamer.

SUSAN

SUSAN poisoned her grandmother's tea ;
  Grandmamma died in agonee.
  Susan's papa was greatly vexed,
And he said to Susan, " My dear, what next ? "

Anonymous.

* By permission of R. H. Russell ; from "Ruthless Rhymes for Heartless Homes," copyright, 1901.

BABY AND MARY

BABY sat on the window-seat;
  Mary pushed Baby into the street;
  Baby's brains were dashed out in the " arey,"
And mother held up her forefinger at Mary.

Anonymous.

THE SUNBEAM

I DINED with a friend in the East, one day,
  Who had no window-sashes;
  A sunbeam through the window came
And burnt his wife to ashes.
" John, sweep your mistress away," said he,
" And bring fresh wine for my friend and me."

Anonymous.

LITTLE WILLIE

LITTLE Willie hung his sister,
  She was dead before we missed her.
  " Willie's always up to tricks!
Ain't he cute?   He's only six! "

Anonymous.

[255]

MARY AMES

PITY now poor Mary Ames,
  Blinded by her brother James;
  Red-hot nails in her eyes he poked, —
I never saw Mary more provoked.

Anonymous.

MUDDLED METAPHORS

By a Moore-ose Melodist

OH, ever thus from childhood's hour,
    I 've seen my fondest hopes recede!
    I never loved a tree or flower
  That did n't trump its partner's lead.

I never nursed a dear gazelle,
  To glad me with its dappled hide,
But when it came to know me well,
  It fell upon the buttered side.

I never taught a cockatoo
  To whistle comic songs profound,
But, just when " Jolly Dogs " it knew,
  It failed for ninepence in the pound.

I never reared a walrus cub
  In my aquarium to plunge,
But, when it learned to love its tub,
  It placidly threw up the sponge!

[256]

I never strove a metaphor
　　To every bosom home to bring
But — just as it had reached the door —
　　It went and cut a pigeon's wing!

Tom Hood, Jr.

VILLON'S STRAIGHT TIP TO
ALL CROSS COVES

" Tout aux tavernes et aux fiells "

SUPPOSE you screeve? or go cheap-jack?
　　Or fake the broads? or fig a nag?
　　Or thimble-rig? or knap a yack?
　　Or pitch a snide? or smash a rag?
　　Suppose you duff? or nose and lag?
Or get the straight, and land your pot?
　　How do you melt the multy swag?
Booze and the blowens cop the lot.

Fiddle, or fence, or mace, or mack;
　　Or moskeneer, or flash the drag;
Dead-lurk a crib, or do a crack;
　　Pad with a slang, or chuck a fag;
　　Bonnet, or tout, or mump and gag;
Rattle the tats, or mark the spot;
　　You cannot bag a single stag;
Booze and the blowens cop the lot.

Suppose you try a different tack,
    And on the square you flash your flag?
At penny-a-lining make your whack,
    Or with the mummers mug and gag?
For nix, for nix the dibbs you bag!
At any graft, no matter what,
    Your merry goblins soon stravag:
Booze and the blowens cop the lot.

The Moral

It's up the spout and Charley Wag
With wipes and tickers and what not
    Until the squeezer nips your scrag,
Booze and the blowens cop the lot.

W. E. Henley.

ODE TO THE HUMAN HEART

BLIND Thamyris, and blind Mæonides,
    Pursue the triumph and partake the gale!
    Drop tears as fast as the Arabian trees,
To point a moral or adorn a tale.

Full many a gem of purest ray serene,
    Thoughts that do often lie too deep for tears,
Like angels' visits, few and far between,
    Deck the long vista of departed years.

Man never is, but always to be bless'd;
    The tenth transmitter of a foolish face,
Like Aaron's serpent, swallows up the rest,
    And makes a sunshine in the shady place.

For man the hermit sigh'd, till woman smiled,
    To waft a feather or to drown a fly,
(In wit a man, simplicity a child,)
    With silent finger pointing to the sky.

But fools rush in where angels fear to tread,
    Far out amid the melancholy main;
As when a vulture on Imaus bred,
    Dies of a rose in aromatic pain.

Laman Blanchard.

LIMERICKS

THERE was an old person of Ware
Who rode on the back of a bear;
    When they said, " Does it trot ? "
    He said : " Certainly not,
It 's a Moppsikon Floppsikon bear."

THERE was an old person of Wick,
Who said, " Tick-a-Tick, Tick-a-Tick,
    Chickabee, Chickabaw,"
    And he said nothing more,
This laconic old person of Wick.

THERE was an old person of Woking,
Whose mind was perverse and provoking;
    He sate on a rail,
    With his head in a pail,
That illusive old person of Woking.

THERE was once a man with a beard
Who said, " It is just as I feared ! —
    Two Owls and a Hen,
    Four Larks and a Wren
Have all built their nests in my beard."

THERE was an old man of Thermopylæ,
Who never did anything properly;
  But they said: "If you choose
  To boil eggs in your shoes,
You cannot remain in Thermopylæ."

THERE was an Old Man who said, "Hush!
I perceive a young bird in this bush!"
  When they said, "Is it small?"
  He replied, "Not at all;
It is four times as big as the bush!"

THERE was an Old Man who supposed
That the street door was partially closed;
  But some very large Rats
  Ate his coats and his hats,
While that futile Old Gentleman dozed.

THERE was an Old Man of Leghorn,
The smallest that ever was born;
  But quickly snapt up he
  Was once by a Puppy,
Who devoured that Old Man of Leghorn.

THERE was an Old Man of Kamschatka
Who possessed a remarkably fat Cur;
  His gait and his waddle
  Were held as a model
To all the fat dogs in Kamschatka.

       Edward Lear.

[*From books printed for the benefit of the New York Fair in aid of the Sanitary Commission,* 1864]

THERE was a gay damsel of Lynn,
  Whose waist was so charmingly thin,
    The dressmaker needed
    A microscope — she did —
To fit this slim person of Lynn.

THERE was a young lady of Milton,
Who was highly disgusted with Stilton;
    When offered a bite,
    She said, "Not a mite!"
That suggestive young lady of Milton.

THERE was a dear lady of Eden,
Who on apples was quite fond of feedin';
    She gave one to Adam,
    Who said, "Thank you, Madam,"
And then both skedaddled from Eden.

THERE was a young lady of Wales,
Who wore her back hair in two tails;
    And a hat on her head
    That was striped black and red,
And studded with ten-penny nails.

[262]

THERE was an old man who said, " Do
Tell me how I 'm to add two and two?
I 'm not very sure
That it does n't make four —
But I fear that is almost too few."

THERE once was a man who said, " How
Shall I manage to carry my cow?
For if I should ask it
To get in my basket,
'T would make such a terrible row."

Anonymous.

———

THERE once was an old man of Lyme
Who married three wives at a time;
When asked, " Why a third?"
He replied, " One 's absurd!
And bigamy, sir, is a crime."

THERE once was a person of Benin,
Who wore clothes not fit to be seen in;
When told that he should n't,
He replied, "Gumscrumrudent!"
A word of inscrutable meanin'.

THERE once was a girl of New York
Whose body was lighter than cork;
   She had to be fed
   For six weeks upon lead,
Before she went out for a walk.

Cosmo Monkhouse.

THERE was a young man who was bitten
  By twenty-two cats and a kitten;
   Sighed he, " It is clear
   My finish is near;
No matter; I 'll die like a Briton ! "

THERE was a princess of Bengal,
Whose mouth was exceedingly small;
   Said she, " It would be
   More easy for me
To do without eating at all ! "

THERE was an old stupid who wrote
The verses above that we quote;
   His want of all sense
   Was something immense,
Which made him a person of note.

Walter Parke.

VERS NONSENSIQUES

À POTSDAM, les totaux absteneurs,
  Comme tant d'autres titotalleurs,
      Sont gloutons, omnivores,
      Nasorubicolores,
Grands manchons, et terribles duffeurs.

Un vieux duc (le meilleur des époux)
Demandait (en lui tâtant le pouls)
      À sa vielle duchesse
      (Qu'un vieux catarrhe oppresse) : —
" Et ton thé, t'a-t-il ôté ta toux ? "

Il naquit près de Choisy-le-Roi ;
Le Latin lui causait de l'effroi ;
      Et les Mathématiques
      Lui donnaient des coliques,
Et le Grec l'enrhûmait.   Ce fut moi.

Il était un gendarme, à Nanteuil,
Qui n'avait qu'une dent et qu'un œil ;
      Mais cet œil solitaire
      Etait plein de mystère ;
Cette dent, d'importance et d'orgueil.

" Cassez-vous, cassez-vous, cassez-vous,
O mer, sur vos froids gris calloux ! "
      Ainsi traduisit Laure
      Au profit d'Isadore
(Bon jeune homme, at son futur epoux.)

[265]

Un marin naufragé (de Doncastre)
Pour prière, au milieu du désastre
  Répétait à genoux
  Ces mots simples et doux : —
" Scintillez, scintillez, petit astre ! "

George du Maurier.

THERE was a young man of Cohoes,*
  Wore tar on the end of his nose ;
    When asked why he done it,
    He said for the fun it
Afforded the men of Cohoes.

Robert J. Burdette.

I'D rather have habits than clothes,
  For that's where my intellect shows.
    And as for my hair,
    Do you think I should care
To comb it at night with my toes ?

I wish that my Room had a Floor ;
I don't so much care for a Door,
    But this walking around
    Without touching the ground
Is getting to be quite a bore !

Gelett Burgess.

* By permission of the author.

[266]

H WAS an indigent Hen,
Who picked up a corn now and then;
She had but one leg
On which she could peg,
And behind her left ear was a wen.

Bruce Porter.

CLEOPATRA, who thought they maligned
her,
Resolved to reform and be kinder;
" If, when pettish," she said,
" I should knock off your head,
Won't you give me some gentle reminder? "

Newton Mackintosh.

WHEN that Seint George hadde sleyne ye
draggon,
He sate him down furninst a flaggon;
And, wit ye well,
Within a spell
He had a bien plaisaunt jag on.

Anonymous.

[267]

THERE was a young lady of Niger
   Who smiled as she rode on a Tiger;
      They came back from the ride
      With the lady inside,
And the smile on the face of the Tiger.

Anonymous.

THERE was a young maid who said, " Why
   Can't I look in my ear with my eye?
      If I give my mind to it,
      I'm sure I can do it,
You never can tell till you try."

INDEX OF TITLES

INDEX OF TITLES

INDEX OF AUTHORS

INDEX OF AUTHORS

INDEX OF FIRST LINES

[291]

Catalog
of
DOVER BOOKS

BOOKS EXPLAINING SCIENCE

(Note: The books listed under this category are general introductions, surveys, reviews, and non-technical expositions of science for the interested layman or scientist who wishes to brush up. Dover also publishes the largest list of inexpensive reprints of books on intermediate and higher mathematics, mathematical physics, engineering, chemistry, astronomy, etc., for the professional mathematician or scientist. For our complete Science Catalog, write Dept. catrr., Dover Publications, Inc., 180 Varick Street, New York 14, N. Y.)

CONCERNING THE NATURE OF THINGS, Sir William· Bragg. Royal Institute Christmas Lectures by Nobel Laureate. Excellent plain-language introduction to gases, molecules, crystal structure, etc. explains "building blocks" of universe, basic properties of matter, with simplest, clearest examples, demonstrations. 32pp. of photos; 57 figures. 244pp. 5⅜ x 8.
T31 Paperbound **$1.35**

MATTER AND LIGHT, THE NEW PHYSICS, Louis de Broglie. Non-technical explanations by a Nobel Laureate of electro-magnetic theory, relativity, wave mechanics, quantum physics, philosophies of science, etc. Simple, yet accurate introduction to work of Planck, Bohr, Einstein, other modern physicists. Only 2 of 12 chapters require mathematics. 300pp. 5⅜ x 8.
T35 Paperbound **$1.60**

THE COMMON ·SENSE OF THE EXACT SCIENCES, W. K. Clifford. For 70 years, Clifford's work has been acclaimed as one of the clearest, yet most precise introductions to mathematical symbolism, measurement, surface boundaries, position, space, motion, mass and force, etc. Prefaces by Bertrand Russell and Karl Pearson. Introduction by James Newman. 130 figures. 249pp. 5⅜ x 8.
T61 Paperbound **$1.60**

THE NATURE OF LIGHT AND COLOUR IN THE OPEN AIR, M. Minnaert. What causes mirages? haloes? "multiple" suns and moons? Professor Minnaert explains these and hundreds of other fascinating natural optical phenomena in simple terms, tells how to observe them, suggests hundreds of experiments. 200 illus; 42 photos. xvi + 362pp.
T196 Paperbound **$1·95**

SPINNING TOPS AND GYROSCOPIC MOTION, John Perry. Classic elementary text on dynamics of rotation treats gyroscopes, tops, how quasi-rigidity is induced in paper disks, smoke rings, chains, etc, by rapid motion, precession, earth's motion, etc. Contains many easy-to-perform experiments. Appendix on practical uses of gyroscopes. 62 figures. 128pp.
T416 Paperbound **$1.00**

A CONCISE HISTORY OF MATHEMATICS, D. Struik. This lucid, easily followed history of mathematics from the Ancient Near East to modern times requires no mathematical background itself, yet introduces both mathematicians and laymen to basic concepts and discoveries and the men who made them. Contains a collection of 31 portraits of eminent mathematicians. Bibliography. xix + 299pp. 5⅜ x 8.
T255 Paperbound **$1.75**

THE RESTLESS UNIVERSE, Max Born. A remarkably clear, thorough exposition of gases, electrons, ions, waves and particles, electronic structure of the atom, nuclear physics, written for the layman by a Nobel Laureate. "Much ·more thorough and deep than most attempts . . . easy and delightful," CHEMICAL AND ENGINEERING NEWS. Includes 7 animated sequences showing motion of molecules, alpha particles, etc. 11 full-page plates of photographs. Total of nearly 600 illus. 315pp. 6⅛ x 9¼.
T412 Paperbound **$2.00**

WHAT IS SCIENCE?, N. Campbell. The role of experiment, the function of mathematics, the nature of scientific laws, the limitations of science, and many other provocative topics are explored without technicalities by an eminent scientist. "Still an excellent introduction to scientific philosophy," H. Margenau in PHYSICS TODAY. 192pp. 5⅜ x 8.
S43 Paperbound **$1.25**

FADS AND FALLACIES IN THE NAME OF SCIENCE, Martin Gardner. The standard account of the various cults, quack systems and delusions which have recently masqueraded as science: hollow earth theory, Atlantis, dianetics, Reich's orgone theory, flying saucers, Bridey Murphy, psionics, irridiagnosis, many other fascinating fallacies that deluded tens of thousands. "Should be read by everyone, scientist and non-scientist alike," R. T. Birge, Prof. Emeritus, Univ. of California; Former President, American Physical Society. Formerly titled, "In the Name of Science." Revised and enlarged edition. x + 365pp. 5⅜ x 8.

T394 Paperbound **$1.50**

THE STUDY OF THE HISTORY OF MATHEMATICS, THE STUDY OF THE HISTORY OF SCIENCE, G. Sarton. Two books bound as one. Both volumes are standard introductions to their fields by an eminent science historian. They discuss problems of historical research, teaching, pitfalls, other matters of interest to the historically oriented writer, teacher, or student. Both have extensive bibliographies. 10 illustrations. 188pp. 5⅜ x 8.   T240 Paperbound **$1.25**

THE PRINCIPLES OF SCIENCE, W. S. Jevons. Unabridged reprinting of a milestone in the development of symbolic logic and other subjects concerning scientific methodology, probability, inferential validity, etc. Also describes Jevons' "logic machine," an early precursor of modern electronic calculators. Preface by E. Nagel. 839pp. 5⅜ x 8.   S446 Paperbound **$2.98**

SCIENCE THEORY AND MAN, Erwin Schroedinger. Complete, unabridged reprinting of "Science and the Human Temperament" plus an additional essay "What is an Elementary Particle?" Nobel Laureate Schroedinger discusses many aspects of modern physics from novel points of view which provide unusual insights for both laymen and physicists. 192 pp. 5⅜ x 8.

T428 Paperbound **$1.35**

BRIDGES AND THEIR BUILDERS, D. B. Steinman & S. R. Watson. Information about ancient, medieval, modern bridges; how they were built; who built them; the structural principles employed; the materials they are built of; etc. Written by one of the world's leading authorities on bridge design and construction. New, revised, expanded edition. 23 photos; 26 line drawings, xvii + 401pp. 5⅜ x 8.   T431 Paperbound **$1.95**

HISTORY OF MATHEMATICS, D. E. Smith. Most comprehensive non-technical history of math in English. In two volumes. Vol. I: A chronological examination of the growth of mathematics from primitive concepts up to 1900. Vol. II: The development of ideas in specific fields and areas, up through elementary calculus. The lives and works of over a thousand mathematicians are covered; thousands of specific historical problems and their solutions are clearly explained. Total of 510 illustrations, 1355pp. 5⅜ x 8. Set boxed in attractive container.   T429, T430 Paperbound, the set **$5.00**

PHILOSOPHY AND THE PHYSICISTS, L. S. Stebbing. A philosopher examines the philosophical implications of modern science by posing a lively critical attack on the popular science expositions of Sir James Jeans and Arthur Eddington. xvi + 295pp. 5⅜ x 8.

T480 Paperbound **$1.65**

ON MATHEMATICS AND MATHEMATICIANS, R. E. Moritz. The first collection of quotations by and about mathematicians in English. 1140 anecdotes, aphorisms, definitions, speculations, etc. give both mathematicians and layman stimulating new insights into what mathematics is, and into the personalities of the great mathematicians from Archimedes to Euler, Gauss, Klein, Weierstrass. Invaluable to teachers, writers. Extensive cross index. 410pp. 5⅜ x 8.

T489 Paperbound **$1.95**

NATURAL SCIENCE, BIOLOGY, GEOLOGY, TRAVEL

A SHORT HISTORY OF ANATOMY AND PHYSIOLOGY FROM THE GREEKS TO HARVEY, C. Singer. A great medical historian's fascinating intermediate account of the slow advance of anatomical and physiological knowledge from pre-scientific times to Vesalius, Harvey. 139 unusually interesting illustrations. 221pp. 5⅜ x 8.   T389 Paperbound **$1.75**

THE BEHAVIOUR AND SOCIAL LIFE OF HONEYBEES, Ronald Ribbands. The most comprehensive, lucid and authoritative book on bee habits, communication, duties, cell life, motivations, etc. "A MUST for every scientist, experimenter, and educator, and a happy and valuable selection for all interested in the honeybee," AMERICAN BEE JOURNAL. 690-item bibliography. 127 illus.; 11 photographic plates. 352pp. 5⅜ x 8⅜.   S410 Clothbound **$4.50**

TRAVELS OF WILLIAM BARTRAM, edited by Mark Van Doren. One of the 18th century's most delightful books, and one of the few first-hand sources of information about American geography, natural history, and anthropology of American Indian tribes of the time. "The mind of a scientist with the soul of a poet," John Livingston Lowes. 13 original illustrations, maps. Introduction by Mark Van Doren. 448pp. 5⅜ x 8.   T326 Paperbound **$2.00**

STUDIES ON THE STRUCTURE AND DEVELOPMENT OF VERTEBRATES, Edwin Goodrich. The definitive study of the skeleton, fins and limbs, head region, divisions of the body cavity, vascular, respiratory, excretory systems, etc., of vertebrates from fish to higher mammals, by the greatest comparative anatomist of recent times. "The standard textbook," JOURNAL OF ANATOMY. 754 illus. 69-page biographical study. 1186-item bibliography. 2 vols. Total of 906pp. 5⅜ x 8.

Vol. I: S449 Paperbound **$2.50**
Vol. II: S450 Paperbound **$2.50**

DOVER BOOKS

THE BIRTH AND DEVELOPMENT OF THE GEOLOGICAL SCIENCES, F. D. Adams. The most complete and thorough history of the earth sciences in print. Covers over 300 geological thinkers and systems; treats fossils, theories of stone growth, paleontology, earthquakes, vulcanists vs. neptunists, odd theories, etc. 91 illustrations, including medieval, Renaissance wood cuts, etc. 632 footnotes and bibliographic notes. 511pp. 308pp. 5⅜ x 8.   T5 Paperbound **$2.00**

FROM MAGIC TO SCIENCE, Charles Singer. A close study of aspects of medical science from the Roman Empire through the Renaissance. The sections on early herbals, and "The Visions of Hildegarde of Bingen," are probably the best studies of these subjects available. 158 unusual classic and medieval illustrations. xxvii + 365pp. 5⅜ x 8.   T390 Paperbound **$2.00**

SAILING ALONE AROUND THE WORLD, Captain Joshua Slocum. Captain Slocum's personal account of his single-handed voyage around the world in a 34-foot boat he rebuilt himself. A classic of both seamanship and descriptive writing. "A nautical equivalent of Thoreau's account," Van Wyck Brooks. 67 illus. 308pp. 5⅜ x 8.   T326 Paperbound **$1.00**

TREES OF THE EASTERN AND CENTRAL UNITED STATES AND CANADA, W. M. Harlow. Standard middle-level guide designed to help you know the characteristics of Eastern trees and identify them at sight by means of an 8-page synoptic key. More than 600 drawings and photographs of twigs, leaves, fruit, other features. xiii + 288pp. 4⅝ x 6½.
T395 Paperbound **$1.35**

FRUIT KEY AND TWIG KEY ("Fruit Key to Northeastern Trees," "Twig Key to Deciduous Woody Plants of Eastern North America"), **W. M. Harlow.** Identify trees in fall, winter, spring. Easy-to-use, synoptic keys, with photographs of every twig and fruit identified. Covers 120 different fruits, 160 different twigs. Over 350 photos. Bibliographies. Glossaries. Total of 143pp. 5⅝ x 8⅜.   T511 Paperbound **$1.25**

INTRODUCTION TO THE STUDY OF EXPERIMENTAL MEDICINE, Claude Bernard. This classic records Bernard's far-reaching efforts to transform physiology into an exact science. It covers problems of vivisection, the limits of physiological experiment, hypotheses in medical experimentation, hundreds of others. Many of his own famous experiments on the liver, the pancreas, etc., are used as examples. Foreword by I. B. Cohen. xxv + 266pp. 5⅜ x 8.
T400 Paperbound **$1.50**

THE ORIGIN OF LIFE, A. I. Oparin. The first modern statement that life evolved from complex nitro-carbon compounds, carefully presented according to modern biochemical knowledge of primary colloids, organic molecules, etc. Begins with historical introduction to the problem of the origin of life. Bibliography. xxv + 270pp. 5⅜ x 8.   S213 Paperbound **$1.75**

A HISTORY OF ASTRONOMY FROM THALES TO KEPLER, J. L. E. Dreyer. The only work in English which provides a detailed picture of man's cosmological views from Egypt, Babylonia, Greece, and Alexandria to Copernicus, Tycho Brahe and Kepler. "Standard reference on Greek astronomy and the Copernican revolution," SKY AND TELESCOPE. Formerly called "A History of Planetary Systems From Thales to Kepler." Bibliography. 21 diagrams. xvii + 430pp. 5⅜ x 8.
S79 Paperbound **$1.98**

URANIUM PROSPECTING, H. L. Barnes. A professional geologist tells you what you need to know. Hundreds of facts about minerals, tests, detectors, sampling, assays, claiming, developing, government regulations, etc. Glossary of technical terms. Annotated bibliography. x + 117pp. 5⅜ x 8.   T309 Paperbound **$1.00**

DE RE METALLICA, Georgius Agricola. All 12 books of this 400 year old classic on metals and metal production, fully annotated, and containing all 289 of the 16th century woodcuts which made the original an artistic masterpiece. A superb gift for geologists, engineers, libraries, artists, historians. Translated by Herbert Hoover & L. H. Hoover. Bibliography, survey of ancient authors. 289 illustrations of the excavating, assaying, smelting, refining, and countless other metal production operations described in the text. 672pp. 6¾ x 10¾. Deluxe library edition.   S6 Clothbound **$10.00**

DE MAGNETE, William Gilbert. A landmark of science by the man who first used the word "electricity," distinguished between static electricity and magnetism, and founded a new science. P. F. Mottelay translation. 90 figures. lix + 368pp. 5⅜ x 8.   S470 Paperbound **$2.00**

THE AUTOBIOGRAPHY OF CHARLES DARWIN AND SELECTED LETTERS, Francis Darwin, ed. Fascinating documents on Darwin's early life, the voyage of the "Beagle," the discovery of evolution, Darwin's thought on mimicry, plant development, vivisection, evolution, many other subjects Letters to Henslow, Lyell, Hooker, Wallace, Kingsley, etc. Appendix. 365pp. 5⅜ x 8.   T479 Paperbound **$1.65**

A WAY OF LIFE AND OTHER SELECTED WRITINGS OF SIR WILLIAM OSLER. 16 of the great physician, teacher and humanist's most inspiring writings on a practical philosophy of life, science and the humanities, and the history of medicine. 5 photographs. Introduction by G. L. Keynes, M.D., F.R.C.S. xx + 278pp. 5⅜ x 8.   T488 Paperbound **$1.50**

LITERATURE

WORLD DRAMA, B. H. Clark. 46 plays from Ancient Greece, Rome, to India, China, Japan. Plays by Aeschylus, Sophocles, Euripides, Aristophanes, Plautus, Marlowe, Jonson, Farquhar, Goldsmith, Cervantes, Molière, Dumas, Goethe, Schiller, Ibsen, many others. One of the most comprehensive collections of important plays from all literature available in English. Over ⅓ of this material is unavailable in any other current edition. Reading lists. 2 volumes. Total of 1364pp. 5⅜ x 8.
Vol. I, T57 Paperbound **$2.00**
Vol. II, T59 Paperbound **$2.00**

MASTERS OF THE DRAMA, John Gassner. The most comprehensive history of the drama in print. Covers more than 800 dramatists and over 2000 plays from the Greeks to modern Western, Near Eastern, Oriental drama. Plot summaries, theatre history, etc. "Best of its kind in English," NEW REPUBLIC. 35 pages of bibliography. 77 photos and drawings. Deluxe edition. xxii + 890pp. 5⅜ x 8.
T100 Clothbound **$5.95**

THE DRAMA OF LUIGI PIRANDELLO, D. Vittorini. All 38 of Pirandello's plays (to 1935) summarized and analyzed in terms of symbolic techniques, plot structure, etc. The only authorized work. Foreword by Pirandello. Biography. Bibliography. xiii + 350pp. 5⅜ x 8.
T435 Paperbound **$1.98**

ARISTOTLE'S THEORY OF POETRY AND THE FINE ARTS, S. H. Butcher, ed. The celebrated "Butcher translation" faced page by page with the Greek text; Butcher's 300-page introduction to Greek poetic, dramatic thought. Modern Aristotelian criticism discussed by John Gassner. lxxvi + 421pp. 5⅜ x 8.
T42 Paperbound **$2.00**

EUGENE O'NEILL: THE MAN AND HIS PLAYS, B. H. Clark. The first published source-book on O'Neill's life and work. Analyzes each play from the early THE WEB up to THE ICEMAN COMETH. Supplies much information about environmental and dramatic influences. ix + 182pp. 5⅜ x 8.
T379 Paperbound **$1.25**

INTRODUCTION TO ENGLISH LITERATURE, B. Dobrée, ed. Most compendious literary aid in its price range. Extensive, categorized bibliography (with entries up to 1949) of more than 5,000 poets, dramatists, novelists, as well as historians, philosophers, economists, religious writers, travellers, and scientists of literary stature. Information about manuscripts, important biographical data. Critical, historical, background works not simply listed, but evaluated. Each volume also contains a long introduction to the period it covers.

Vol. I: **THE BEGINNINGS OF ENGLISH LITERATURE TO SKELTON, 1509, W. L. Renwick. H. Orton.** 450pp. 5⅛ x 7⅛.
T75 Clothbound **$3.50**

Vol. II: **THE ENGLISH RENAISSANCE, 1510-1688, V. de Sola Pinto.** 381pp. 5⅛ x 7⅛.
T76 Clothbound **$3.50**

Vol. III: **THE AUGUSTANS AND ROMANTICS, 1689-1830, H. Dyson, J. Butt.** 320pp. 5⅛ x 7⅛.
T77 Clothbound **$3.50**

Vol. IV: **THE VICTORIANS AND AFTER, 1830-1914, E. Batho, B. Dobrée.** 360pp. 5⅛ x 7⅛.
T78 Clothbound **$3.50**

EPIC AND ROMANCE, W. P. Ker. The standard survey of Medieval epic and romance by a foremost authority on Medieval literature. Covers historical background, plot, literary analysis, significance of Teutonic epics, Icelandic sagas, Beowulf, French chansons de geste, the Niebelungenlied, Arthurian romances, much more. 422pp. 5⅜ x 8.
T355 Paperbound **$1.95**

THE HEART OF EMERSON'S JOURNALS, Bliss Perry, ed. Emerson's most intimate thoughts, impressions, records of conversations with Channing, Hawthorne, Thoreau, etc., carefully chosen from the 10 volumes of The Journals. "The essays do not reveal the power of Emerson's mind . . . as do these hasty and informal writings," N. Y. TIMES. Preface by B. Perry. 370pp. 5⅜ x 8.
T447 Paperbound **$1.85**

A SOURCE BOOK IN THEATRICAL HISTORY, A. M. Nagler. (Formerly, "Sources of Theatrical History.") Over 300 selected passages by contemporary observers tell about styles of acting, direction, make-up, scene designing, etc., in the theatre's great periods from ancient Greece to the Théâtre Libre. "Indispensable complement to the study of drama," EDUCATIONAL THEATRE JOURNAL. Prof. Nagler, Yale Univ. School of Drama, also supplies notes, references. 85 illustrations. 611pp. 5⅜ x 8.
T515 Paperbound **$2.75**

THE ART OF THE STORY-TELLER, M. L. Shedlock. Regarded as the finest, most helpful book on telling stories to children, by a great story-teller. How to catch, hold, recapture attention; how to choose material; many other aspects. Also includes: a 99-page selection of Miss Shedlock's most successful stories; extensive bibliography of other stories. xxi + 320pp. 5⅜ x 8.
T245 Clothbound **$3.50**

THE DEVIL'S DICTIONARY, Ambrose Bierce. Over 1000 short, ironic definitions in alphabetical order, by America's greatest satirist in the classical tradition. "Some of the most gorgeous witticisms in the English language," H. L. Mencken. 144pp. 5⅜ x 8.
T487 Paperbound **$1.00**

MUSIC

A DICTIONARY OF HYMNOLOGY, John Julian. More than 30,000 entries on individual hymns, their authorship, textual variations, location of texts, dates and circumstances of composition, denominational and ritual usages, the biographies of more than 9,000 hymn writers, essays on important topics such as children's hymns and Christmas carols, and hundreds of thousands of other important facts about hymns which are virtually impossible to find anywhere else. Convenient alphabetical listing, and a 200-page double-columned index of first lines enable you to track down virtually any hymn ever written. Total of 1786pp. 6¼ x 9¼. 2 volumes. **T133. The Set, Clothbound $15.00**

STRUCTURAL HEARING, TONAL COHERENCE IN MUSIC, Felix Salzer. Extends the well-known Schenker approach to include modern music, music of the middle ages, and Renaissance music. Explores the phenomenon of tonal organization by discussing more than 500 compositions, and offers unusual new insights into the theory of composition and musical relationships. "The foundation on which all teaching in music theory has been based at this college," Leopold Mannes, President, The Mannes College of Music. Total of 658pp. 6½ x 9¼. 2 volumes. **S418 The set, Clothbound $8.00**

A GENERAL HISTORY OF MUSIC, Charles Burney. The complete history of music from the Greeks up to 1789 by the 18th century musical historian who personally knew the great Baroque composers. Covers sacred and secular, vocal and instrumental, operatic and symphonic music; treats theory, notation, forms, instruments; discusses composers, performers, important works. Invaluable as a source of information on the period for students, historians, musicians. "Surprisingly few of Burney's statements have been invalidated by modern research . . . still of great value," NEW YORK TIMES. Edited and corrected by Frank Mercer. 35 figures. 1915pp. 5½ x 8½. 2 volumes. **T36 The set, Clothbound $12.50**

JOHANN SEBASTIAN BACH, Phillip Spitta. Recognized as one of the greatest accomplishments of musical scholarship and far and away the definitive coverage of Bach's works. Hundreds of individual pieces are analyzed. Major works, such as the B Minor Mass and the St. Matthew Passion are examined in minute detail. Spitta also deals with the works of Buxtehude, Pachelbel, and others of the period. Can be read with profit even by those without a knowledge of the technicalities of musical composition. "Unchallenged as the last word on one of the supreme geniuses of music," John Barkham, SATURDAY REVIEW SYNDICATE. Total of 1819pp. 5⅜ x 8. 2 volumes. **T252 The set, Clothbound $10.00**

HISTORY

THE IDEA OF PROGRESS, J. B. Bury. Prof. Bury traces the evolution of a central concept of Western civilization in Greek, Roman, Medieval, and Renaissance thought to its flowering in the 17th and 18th centuries. Introduction by Charles Beard. xl + 357pp. 5⅜ x 8.
T39 Clothbound $3.95
T40 Paperbound $1.95

THE ANCIENT GREEK HISTORIANS, J. B. Bury. Greek historians such as Herodotus, Thucydides, Xenophon; Roman historians such as Tacitus, Caesar, Livy; scores of others fully analyzed in terms of sources, concepts, influences, etc., by a great scholar and historian. 291pp. 5⅜ x 8. **T397 Paperbound $1.50**

HISTORY OF THE LATER ROMAN EMPIRE, J. B. Bury. The standard work on the Byzantine Empire from 395 A.D. to the death of Justinian in 565 A.D., by the leading Byzantine scholar of our time. Covers political, social, cultural, theological, military history. Quotes contemporary documents extensively. "Most unlikely that it will ever be superseded," Glanville Downey, Dumbarton Oaks Research Library. Genealogical tables. 5 maps. Bibliography. 2 vols. Total of 965pp. 5⅜ x 8. **T398, T399 Paperbound, the set $4.00**

GARDNER'S PHOTOGRAPHIC SKETCH BOOK OF THE CIVIL WAR, Alexander Gardner. One of the rarest and most valuable Civil War photographic collections exactly reproduced for the first time since 1866. Scenes of Manassas, Bull Run, Harper's Ferry, Appomattox, Mechanicsville, Fredericksburg, Gettysburg, etc.; battle ruins, prisons, arsenals, a slave pen, fortifications; Lincoln on the field, officers, men, corpses. By one of the most famous pioneers in documentary photography. Original copies of the "Sketch Book" sold for $425 in 1952. Introduction by E. Bleiler. 100 full-page 7 x 10 photographs (original size). 244pp. 10¾ x 8½
T476 Clothbound $6.00

THE WORLD'S GREAT SPEECHES, L. Copeland and L. Lamm, eds. 255 speeches from Pericles to Churchill, Dylan Thomas. Invaluable as a guide to speakers; fascinating as history past and present; a source of much difficult-to-find material. Includes an extensive section of informal and humorous speeches. 3 indices: Topic, Author, Nation. xx + 745pp. 5⅜ x 8.
T468 Paperbound $2.49

FOUNDERS OF THE MIDDLE AGES, E. K. Rand. The best non-technical discussion of the transformation of Latin paganism into medieval civilization. Tertullian, Gregory, Jerome, Boethius, Augustine, the Neoplatonists, other crucial figures, philosophies examined. Excellent for the intelligent non-specialist. "Extraordinarily accurate," Richard McKeon, THE NATION. ix + 365pp. 5⅜ x 8. **T369 Paperbound $1.85**

THE POLITICAL THOUGHT OF PLATO AND ARISTOTLE, Ernest Barker. The standard, comprehensive exposition of Greek political thought. Covers every aspect of the "Republic" and the "Politics" as well as minor writings, other philosophers, theorists of the period, and the later history of Greek political thought. Unabridged edition. 584pp. 5⅜ x 8.
T521 Paperbound **$1.85**

PHILOSOPHY

THE GIFT OF LANGUAGE, M. Schlauch. (Formerly, "The Gift of Tongues.") A sound, middle-level treatment of linguistic families, word histories, grammatical processes, semantics, language taboos, word-coining of Joyce, Cummings, Stein, etc. 232 bibliographical notes. 350pp. 5⅜ x 8.
T243 Paperbound **$1.85**

THE PHILOSOPHY OF HEGEL, W. T. Stace. The first work in English to give a complete and connected view of Hegel's entire system. Especially valuable to those who do not have time to study the highly complicated original texts, yet want an accurate presentation by a most reputable scholar of one of the most influential 19th century thinkers. Includes a 14 x 20 fold-out chart of Hegelian system. 536pp. 5⅜ x 8.
T254 Paperbound **$2.00**

ARISTOTLE, A. E. Taylor. A lucid, non-technical account of Aristotle written by a foremost Platonist. Covers life and works; thought on matter, form, causes, logic, God, physics, metaphysics, etc. Bibliography. New index compiled for this edition. 128pp. 5⅜ x 8.
T280 Paperbound **$1.00**

GUIDE TO PHILOSOPHY, C. E. M. Joad. This basic work describes the major philosophic problems and evaluates the answers propounded by great philosophers from the Greeks to Whitehead, Russell. "The finest introduction," BOSTON TRANSCRIPT. Bibliography, 592pp. 5⅜ x 8.
T297 Paperbound **$2.00**

LANGUAGE AND MYTH, E. Cassirer. Cassirer's brilliant demonstration that beneath both language and myth lies an unconscious "grammar" of experience whose categories and canons are not those of logical thought. Introduction and translation by Susanne Langer. Index. x + 103pp. 5⅜ x 8.
T51 Paperbound **$1.25**

SUBSTANCE AND FUNCTION, EINSTEIN'S THEORY OF RELATIVITY, E. Cassirer. This double volume contains the German philosopher's profound philosophical formulation of the differences between traditional logic and the new logic of science. Number, space, energy, relativity, many other topics are treated in detail. Authorized translation by W. C. and M. C. Swabey. xii + 465pp. 5⅜ x 8.
T50 Paperbound **$2.00**

THE PHILOSOPHICAL WORKS OF DESCARTES. The definitive English edition, in two volumes, of all major philosophical works and letters of René Descartes, father of modern philosophy of knowledge and science. Translated by E. S. Haldane and G. Ross. Introductory notes. Total of 842pp. 5⅜ x 8.
T71 Vol. 1, Paperbound **$2.00**
T72 Vol. 2, Paperbound **$2.00**

ESSAYS IN EXPERIMENTAL LOGIC, J. Dewey. Based upon Dewey's theory that knowledge implies a judgment which in turn implies an inquiry, these papers consider such topics as the thought of Bertrand Russell, pragmatism, the logic of values, antecedents of thought, data and meanings. 452pp. 5⅜ x 8.
T73 Paperbound **$1.95**

THE PHILOSOPHY OF HISTORY, G. W. F. Hegel. This classic of Western thought is Hegel's detailed formulation of the thesis that history is not chance but a rational process, the realization of the Spirit of Freedom. Translated and introduced by J. Sibree. Introduction by C. Hegel. Special introduction for this edition by Prof. Carl Friedrich, Harvard University. xxxix + 447pp. 5⅜ x 8.
T112 Paperbound **$1.85**

THE WILL TO BELIEVE and HUMAN IMMORTALITY, W. James. Two of James's most profound investigations of human belief in God and immortality, bound as one volume. Both are powerful expressions of James's views on chance vs. determinism, pluralism vs. monism, will and intellect, arguments for survival after death, etc. Two prefaces. 429pp. 5⅜ x 8.
T294 Clothbound **$3.75**
T291 Paperbound **$1.65**

INTRODUCTION TO SYMBOLIC LOGIC, S. Langer. A lucid, general introduction to modern logic, covering forms, classes, the use of symbols, the calculus of propositions, the Boole-Schroeder and the Russell-Whitehead systems, etc. "One of the clearest and simplest introductions," MATHEMATICS GAZETTE. Second, enlarged, revised edition. 368pp. 5⅜ x 8.
S164 Paperbound **$1.75**

MIND AND THE WORLD-ORDER, C. I. Lewis. Building upon the work of Peirce, James, and Dewey, Professor Lewis outlines a theory of knowledge in terms of "conceptual pragmatism," and demonstrates why the traditional understanding of the a priori must be abandoned. Appendices. xiv + 446pp. 5⅜ x 8.
T359 Paperbound **$1.95**

THE GUIDE FOR THE PERPLEXED, M. Maimonides One of the great philosophical works of all time, Maimonides' formulation of the meeting-ground between Old Testament and Aristotelian thought is essential to anyone interested in Jewish, Christian, and Moslem thought in the Middle Ages. 2nd revised edition of the Friedlander translation. Extensive introduction. lix + 414pp. 5⅜ x 8.
T351 Paperbound **$1.85**

THE PHILOSOPHICAL WRITINGS OF PEIRCE, J. Buchler, ed. (Formerly, "The Philosophy of Peirce.") This carefully integrated selection of Peirce's papers is considered the best coverage of the complete thought of one of the greatest philosophers of modern times. Covers Peirce's work on the theory of signs, pragmatism, epistemology, symbolic logic, the scientific method, chance, etc. xvi + 386pp. 5 ⅜ x 8.　　　　　　　　T216 Clothbound **$5.00**
　　　　　　　　　　　　　　　　　　　　　　　　　　　　T217 Paperbound **$1.95**

HISTORY OF ANCIENT PHILOSOPHY, W. Windelband. Considered the clearest survey of Greek and Roman philosophy. Examines Thales, Anaximander, Anaximenes, Heraclitus, the Eleatics, Empedocles, the Pythagoreans, the Sophists, Socrates, Democritus, Stoics, Epicureans, Sceptics, Neo-platonists, etc. 50 pages on Plato; 70 on Aristotle. 2nd German edition tr. by H. E. Cushman. xv + 393pp. 5⅜ x 8.　　　　　　　　　　　　　T357 Paperbound **$1.75**

INTRODUCTION TO SYMBOLIC LOGIC AND ITS APPLICATIONS, R. Carnap. A comprehensive, rigorous introduction to modern logic by perhaps its greatest living master. Includes demonstrations of applications in mathematics, physics, biology. "Of the rank of a masterpiece," Z. für Mathematik und ihre Grenzgebiete. Over 300 exercises. xvi + 241pp. 5⅜ x 8.　　　　　　　　　　　　　　　　　Clothbound **$4.00**
　　　　　　　　　　　　　　　　　　　　　　　　　　　　S453 Paperbound **$1.85**

SCEPTICISM AND ANIMAL FAITH, G. Santayana. Santayana's unusually lucid exposition of the difference between the independent existence of objects and the essence our mind attributes to them, and of the necessity of scepticism as a form of belief and animal faith as a necessary condition of knowledge. Discusses belief, memory, intuition, symbols, etc. xii + 314pp. 5⅜ x 8.　　　　　　　　　　　　　　　　　T235 Clothbound **$3.50**
　　　　　　　　　　　　　　　　　　　　　　　　　　　　T236 Paperbound **$1.50**

THE ANALYSIS OF MATTER, B. Russell. With his usual brilliance, Russell analyzes physics, causality, scientific inference, Weyl's theory, tensors, invariants, periodicity, etc. in order to discover the basic concepts of scientific thought about matter. "Most thorough treatment of the subject," THE NATION. Introduction. 8 figures. viii + 408pp. 5⅜ x 8.
　　　　　　　　　　　　　　　　　　　　　　　　　　　　T231 Paperbound **$1.95**

THE SENSE OF BEAUTY, G. Santayana. This important philosophical study of why, when, and how beauty appears, and what conditions must be fulfilled, is in itself a revelation of the beauty of language. "It is doubtful if a better treatment of the subject has since appeared," PEABODY JOURNAL. ix + 275pp. 5⅜ x 8.　　　　　　　T238 Paperbound **$1.00**

THE CHIEF WORKS OF SPINOZA. In two volumes. Vol. I: The Theologico-Political Treatise and the Political Treatise. Vol. II: On the Improvement of Understanding, The Ethics, and Selected Letters. The permanent and enduring ideas in these works on God, the universe, religion, society, etc., have had tremendous impact on later philosophical works. Introduction. Total of 862pp. 5⅜ x 8.　　　　　　　T249 Vol. I, Paperbound **$1.50**
　　　　　　　　　　　　　　　　　　　　　　　　T250 Vol. II, Paperbound **$1.50**

TRAGIC SENSE OF LIFE, M. de Unamuno. The acknowledged masterpiece of one of Spain's most influential thinkers. Between the despair at the inevitable death of man and all his works, and the desire for immortality, Unamuno finds a "saving incertitude." Called "a masterpiece," by the ENCYCLOPAEDIA BRITANNICA. xxx + 332pp. 5⅜ x 8.
　　　　　　　　　　　　　　　　　　　　　　　　　　　　T257 Paperbound **$1.95**

EXPERIENCE AND NATURE, John Dewey. The enlarged, revised edition of the Paul Carus lectures (1925). One of Dewey's clearest presentations of the philosophy of empirical naturalism which reestablishes the continuity between "inner" experience and "outer" nature. These lectures are among the most significant ever delivered by an American philosopher. 457pp. 5⅜ x 8.　　　　　　　　　　　　　　T471 Paperbound **$1.85**

PHILOSOPHY AND CIVILIZATION IN THE MIDDLE AGES, M. de Wulf. A semi-popular survey of medieval intellectual life, religion, philosophy, science, the arts, etc. that covers feudalism vs. Catholicism, rise of the universities, mendicant orders, and similar topics. Bibliography. viii + 320pp. 5⅜ x 8.　　　　　　　　　　　　T284 Paperbound **$1.75**

AN INTRODUCTION TO SCHOLASTIC PHILOSOPHY, M. de Wulf. (Formerly, "Scholasticism Old and New.") Prof. de Wulf covers the central scholastic tradition from St. Anselm, Albertus Magnus, Thomas Aquinas, up to Suarez in the 17th century; and then treats the modern revival of scholasticism, the Louvain position, relations with Kantianism and positivism, etc. xvi + 271pp. 5⅜ x 8.　　　　　　　　　T296 Clothbound **$3.50**
　　　　　　　　　　　　　　　　　　　　　　　　　　　　T283 Paperbound **$1.75**

A HISTORY OF MODERN PHILOSOPHY, H. Höffding. An exceptionally clear and detailed coverage of Western philosophy from the Renaissance to the end of the 19th century. Both major and minor figures are examined in terms of theory of knowledge, logic, cosmology, psychology. Covers Pomponazzi, Bodin, Boehme, Telesius, Bruno, Copernicus, Descartes, Spinoza, Hobbes, Locke, Hume, Kant, Fichte, Schopenhauer, Mill, Spencer, Langer, scores of others. A standard reference work. 2 volumes. Total of 1159pp. 5⅜ x 8.　　　　T117 Vol. 1, Paperbound **$2.00**
　　　　　　　　　　　　　　　　　　　　　　　　T118 Vol. 2, Paperbound **$2.00**

LANGUAGE, TRUTH AND LOGIC, A. J. Ayer. The first full-length development of Logical Positivism in English. Building on the work of Schlick, Russell, Carnap, and the Vienna school, Ayer presents the tenets of one of the most important systems of modern philosophical thought. 160pp. 5⅜ x 8.　　　　　　　　　T10 Paperbound **$1.25**

ORIENTALIA AND RELIGION

THE MYSTERIES OF MITHRA, F. Cumont. The great Belgian scholar's definitive study of the Persian mystery religion that almost vanquished Christianity in the ideological struggle for the Roman Empire. A masterpiece of scholarly detection that reconstructs secret doctrines, organization, rites. Mithraic art is discussed and analyzed. 70 illus. 239pp. 5⅜ x 8.
T323 Paperbound **$1.85**

CHRISTIAN AND ORIENTAL PHILOSOPHY OF ART. A. K. Coomaraswamy. The late art historian and orientalist discusses artistic symbolism, the role of traditional culture in enriching art, medieval art, folklore, philosophy of art, other similar topics. Bibliography. 148pp. 5⅜ x 8.
T378 Paperbound **$1.25**

TRANSFORMATION OF NATURE IN ART, A. K. Coomaraswamy. A basic work on Asiatic religious art. Includes discussions of religious art in Asia and Medieval Europe (exemplified by Meister Eckhart), the origin and use of images in Indian art, Indian Medieval aesthetic manuals, and other fascinating, little known topics. Glossaries of Sanskrit and Chinese terms. Bibliography. 41pp. of notes. 245pp. 5⅜ x 8.
T368 Paperbound **$1.75**

ORIENTAL RELIGIONS IN ROMAN PAGANISM, F. Cumont. This well-known study treats the ecstatic cults of Syria and Phrygia (Cybele, Attis, Adonis, their orgies and mutilatory rites); the mysteries of Egypt (Serapis, Isis, Osiris); Persian dualism; Mithraic cults; Hermes Trismegistus, Ishtar, Astarte, etc. and their influence on the religious thought of the Roman Empire. Introduction. 55pp. of notes; extensive bibliography. xxiv + 298pp. 5⅜ x 8.
T321 Paperbound **$1.75**

ANTHROPOLOGY, SOCIOLOGY, AND PSYCHOLOGY

PRIMITIVE MAN AS PHILOSOPHER, P. Radin. A standard anthropological work based on Radin's investigations of the Winnebago, Maori, Batak, Zuni, other primitive tribes. Describes primitive thought on the purpose of life, marital relations, death, personality, gods, etc. Extensive selections of õriginal primitive documents. Bibliography. xviii + 420pp. 5⅜ x 8.
T392 Paperbound **$2.00**

PRIMITIVE RELIGION, P. Radin. Radin's thoroughgoing treatment of supernatural beliefs, shamanism, initiations, religious expression, etc. in primitive societies. Arunta, Ashanti, Aztec, Bushman, Crow, Fijian, many other tribes examined. "Excellent," NATURE. New preface by the author. Bibliographic notes. x + 322pp. 5⅜ x 8. T393 Paperbound **$1.85**

SEX IN PSYCHO-ANALYSIS, S. Ferenczi. (Formerly, "Contributions to Psycho-analysis.") 14 selected papers on impotence, transference, analysis and children, dreams, obscene words, homosexuality, paranoia, etc. by an associate of Freud. Also included: THE DEVELOPMENT OF PSYCHO-ANALYSIS, by Ferenczi and Otto Rank. Two books bound as one. Total of 406pp. 5⅜ x 8. T324 Paperbound **$1.85**

THE PRINCIPLES OF PSYCHOLOGY, William James. The complete text of the famous "long course," one of the great books of Western thought. An almost incredible amount of information about psychological processes, the stream of consciousness, habit, time perception, memory, emotions, reason, consciousness of self, abnormal phenomena, and similar topics. Based on James's own discoveries integrated with the work of Descartes, Locke, Hume, Royce, Wundt, Berkeley, Lotse, Herbart, scores of others. "A classic of interpretation," PSYCHIATRIC QUARTERLY. 94 illus. 1408pp. 2 volumes. 5⅜ x 8.
T381 Vol. 1, Paperbound **$2.50**
T382 Vol. 2, Paperbound **$2.50**

THE POLISH PEASANT IN EUROPE AND AMERICA, W. I. Thomas, F. Znaniecki. Monumental sociological study of peasant primary groups (family and community) and the disruptions produced by a new industrial system and emigration to America, by two of the foremost sociologists of recent times. One of the most important works in sociological thought. Includes hundreds of pages of primary documentation; point by point analysis of causes of social decay, breakdown of morality, crime, drunkenness, prostitution, etc. 2nd revised edition. 2 volumes. Total of 2250pp. 6 x 9. T478 2 volume set, Clothbound **$12.50**

FOLKWAYS, W. G. Sumner. The great Yale sociologist's detailed exposition of thousands of social, sexual, and religious customs in hundreds of cultures from ancient Greece to Modern Western societies. Preface by A. G. Keller. Introduction by William Lyon Phelps. 705pp. 5⅜ x 8. S508 Paperbound **$2.49**

BEYOND PSYCHOLOGY, Otto Rank. The author, an early associate of Freud, uses psychoanalytic techniques of myth-analysis to explore ultimates of human existence. Treats love, immortality, the soul, sexual identity, kingship, sources of state power, many other topics which illuminate the irrational basis of human existence. 291pp. 5⅜ x 8. T485 Paperbound **$1.75**

ILLUSIONS AND DELUSIONS OF THE SUPERNATURAL AND THE OCCULT, D. H. Rawcliffe. A rational, scientific examination of crystal gazing, automatic writing, table turning, stigmata, the Indian rope trick, dowsing, telepathy, clairvoyance, ghosts, ESP, PK, thousands of other supposedly occult phenomena. Originally titled "The Psychology of the Occult." 14 illustrations. 551pp. 5⅜ x 8. T503 Paperbound **$2.00**

DOVER BOOKS

YOGA: A SCIENTIFIC EVALUATION, Kovoor T. Behanan. A scientific study of the physiological and psychological effects of Yoga discipline, written under the auspices of the Yale University Institute of Human Relations. Foreword by W. A. Miles, Yale Univ. 17 photographs. 290pp. 5⅜ x 8.   T505 Paperbound **$1.65**

HOAXES, C. D. MacDougall. Delightful, entertaining, yet scholarly exposition of how hoaxes start, why they succeed, documented with stories of hundreds of the most famous hoaxes. "A stupendous collection . . . and shrewd analysis, "NEW YORKER. New, revised edition. 54 photographs. 320pp. 5⅜ x 8.   T465 Paperbound **$1.75**

CREATIVE POWER: THE EDUCATION OF YOUTH IN THE CREATIVE ARTS, Hughes Mearns. Named by the National Education Association as one of the 20 foremost books on education in recent times. Tells how to help children express themselves in drama, poetry, music, art, develop latent creative power. Should be read by every parent, teacher. New, enlarged, revised edition. Introduction. 272pp. 5⅜ x 8.   T490 Paperbound **$1.50**

LANGUAGES

NEW RUSSIAN-ENGLISH, ENGLISH-RUSSIAN DICTIONARY, M. A. O'Brien. Over 70,000 entries in new orthography! Idiomatic usages, colloquialisms. One of the few dictionaries that indicate accent changes in conjugation and declension. "One of the best," Prof. E. J. Simmons, Cornell. First names, geographical terms, bibliography, many other features. 738pp. 4½ x 6¼.
T208 Paperbound **$2.00**

MONEY CONVERTER AND TIPPING GUIDE FOR EUROPEAN TRAVEL, C. Vomacka. Invaluable, handy source of currency regulations, conversion tables, tipping rules, postal rates, much other travel information for every European country plus Israel, Egypt and Turkey. 128pp. 3½ x 5¼.
T260 Paperbound **60¢**

MONEY CONVERTER AND TIPPING GUIDE FOR TRAVEL IN THE AMERICAS (including the United States and Canada), **C. Vomacka.** The information you need for informed and confident travel in the Americas: money conversion tables, tipping guide, postal, telephone rates, etc. 128pp. 3½ x 5¼.   T261 Paperbound **65¢**

DUTCH-ENGLISH, ENGLISH-DUTCH DICTIONARY, F. G. Renier. The most convenient, practical Dutch-English dictionary on the market. New orthography. More than 60,000 entries: idioms, compounds, technical terms, etc. Gender of nouns indicated. xviii + 571pp. 5½ x 6¼.
T224 Clothbound **$2.50**

LEARN DUTCH!, F. G. Renier. The most satisfactory and easily-used grammar of modern Dutch. Used and recommended by the Fulbright Committee in the Netherlands. Over 1200 simple exercises lead to mastery of spoken and written Dutch. Dutch-English, English-Dutch vocabularies. 181pp. 4¼ x 7¼.   T441 Clothbound **$1.75**

PHRASE AND SENTENCE DICTIONARY OF SPOKEN RUSSIAN, English-Russian, Russian-English. Based on phrases and complete sentences, rather than isolated words; recognized as one of the best methods of learning the idiomatic speech of a country. Over 11,500 entries, indexed by single words, with more than 32,000 English and Russian sentences and phrases, in immediately usable form. Probably the largest list ever published. Shows accent changes in conjugation and declension; irregular forms listed in both alphabetical place and under main form of word. 15,000 word introduction covering Russian sounds, writing, grammar, syntax. 15-page appendix of geographical names, money, important signs, given names, foods, special Soviet terms, etc. Travellers, businessmen, students, government employees have found this their best source for Russian expressions. Originally published as U.S. Government Technical Manual TM 30-944. iv + 573pp. 5⅝ x 8⅜.   T496 Paperbound **$2.75**

PHRASE AND SENTENCE DICTIONARY OF SPOKEN SPANISH, Spanish-English, English-Spanish. Compiled from spoken Spanish, emphasizing idiom and colloquial usage in both Castilian and Latin-American. More than 16,000 entries containing over 25,000 idioms—the largest list of idiomatic constructions ever published. Complete sentences given, indexed under single words —language in immediately usable form, for travellers, businessmen, students, etc. 25-page introduction provides rapid survey of sounds, grammar, syntax, with full consideration of irregular verbs. Especially apt in modern treatment of phrases and structure. 17-page glossary gives translations of geographical names, money values, numbers, national holidays, important street signs, useful expressions of high frequency, plus unique 7-page glossary of Spanish and Spanish-American foods and dishes. Originally published as U.S. Government Technical Manual TM 30-900. iv + 513pp. 5⅝ x 8⅜.   T495 Paperbound **$1.75**

SAY IT language phrase books

"SAY IT" in the foreign language of your choice! We have sold over ½ million copies of these popular, useful language books. They will not make you an expert linguist overnight, but they do cover most practical matters of everyday life abroad.

Over 1000 useful phrases, expressions, with additional variants, substitutions.

Modern! Useful! Hundreds of phrases not available in other texts: "Nylon," "air-conditioned," etc.

The ONLY inexpensive phrase book **completely indexed.** Everything is available at a flip of your finger, ready for use.

Prepared by native linguists, travel experts.

Based on years of travel experience abroad.

This handy phrase book may be used by itself, or it may supplement any other text or course; it provides a living element. Used by many colleges and institutions: Hunter College; Barnard College; Army Ordnance School, Aberdeen; and many others.

Available, 1 book per language:

Danish (T818) 75¢
Dutch T(817) 75¢
English (for German-speaking people) (T801) 60¢
English (for Italian-speaking people) (T816) 60¢
English (for Spanish-speaking people) (T802) 60¢
Esperanto (T820) 75¢
French (T803) 60¢
German (T804) 60¢
Modern Greek (T813) 75¢
Hebrew (T805) 60¢

Italian (T806) 60¢
Japanese (T807) 60¢
Norwegian (T814) 75¢
Russian (T810) 75¢
Spanish (T811) 60¢
Turkish (T821) 75¢
Yiddish (T815) 75¢
Swedish (T812) 75¢
Polish (T808) 75¢
Portuguese (T809) 75¢

LISTEN & LEARN language record sets

LISTEN & LEARN is the only language record course designed especially to meet your travel needs, or help you learn essential foreign language quickly by yourself, or in conjunction with any school course, by means of the automatic association method. Each set contains three 33⅓ rpm long-playing records — 1½ hours of recorded speech by eminent native speakers who are professors at Columbia, N.Y.U., Queens College and other leading universities. The sets are priced far below other sets of similar quality, yet they contain many special features not found in other record sets:

* Over 800 selected phrases and sentences, a basic vocabulary of over 3200 words.
* Both English and foreign language recorded; with a pause for your repetition.
* Designed for persons with limited time; no time wasted on material you cannot use immediately.
* Living, modern expressions that answer modern needs: drugstore items, "air-conditioned," etc.
* 128-196 page manuals contain everything on the records, plus simple pronunciation guides.
* Manual is fully indexed; find the phrase you want instantly.
* High fidelity recording—equal to any records costing up to $6 each.

The phrases on these records cover 41 different categories useful to the traveller or student interested in learning the living, spoken language: greetings, introductions, making yourself understood, passing customs, planes, trains, boats, buses, taxis, nightclubs, restaurants, menu items, sports, concerts, cameras, automobile travel, repairs, drugstores, doctors, dentists, medicines, barber shops, beauty parlors, laundries, many, many more.

"Excellent . . . among the very best on the market," Prof. Mario Pei, Dept. of Romance Languages, Columbia University. "Inexpensive and well-done . . . an ideal present," CHICAGO SUNDAY TRIBUNE. "More genuinely helpful than anything of its kind which I have previously encountered," Sidney Clark, well-known author of "ALL THE BEST" travel books. Each set contains 3 33⅓ rpm pure vinyl records, 128- 196 page with full record text, and album. One language per set. LISTEN & LEARN record sets are now available in—

FRENCH   the set $4.95   GERMAN   the set $4.95
ITALIAN   the set $4.95   SPANISH   the set $4.95
RUSSIAN   the set $5.95   JAPANESE * the set $5.95
* Available Sept. 1, 1959

UNCONDITIONAL GUARANTEE: Dover Publications stands behind every Listen and Learn record set. If you are dissatisfied with these sets for any reason whatever, return them within 10 days and your money will be refunded in full.

ART HISTORY

STICKS AND STONES, Lewis Mumford. An examination of forces influencing American architecture: the medieval tradition in early New England, the classical influence in Jefferson's time, the Brown Decades, the imperial facade, the machine age, etc. "A truly remarkable book," SAT. REV. OF LITERATURE. 2nd revised edition. 21 illus. xvii + 228pp. 5⅜ x 8.
T202 Paperbound **$1.60**

THE AUTOBIOGRAPHY OF AN IDEA, Louis Sullivan. The architect whom Frank Lloyd Wright called "the master," records the development of the theories that revolutionized America's skyline. 34 full-page plates of Sullivan's finest work. New introduction by R. M. Line. xiv + 335pp. 5⅜ x 8. T281 Paperbound **$1.85**

THE MATERIALS AND TECHNIQUES OF MEDIEVAL PAINTING, D. V. Thompson. An invaluable study of carriers and grounds, binding media, pigments, metals used in painting, al fresco and al secco techniques, burnishing, etc. used by the medieval masters. Preface by Bernard Berenson. 239pp. 5⅜ x 8. T327 Paperbound **$1.85**

PRINCIPLES OF ART HISTORY, H. Wölfflin. This remarkably instructive work demonstrates the tremendous change in artistic conception from the 14th to the 18th centuries, by analyzing 164 works by Botticelli, Dürer, Hobbema, Holbein, Hals, Titian, Rembrandt, Vermeer, etc., and pointing out exactly what is meant by "baroque," "classic," "primitive," "picturesque," and other basic terms of art history and criticism. "A remarkable lesson in the art of seeing," SAT. REV. OF LITERATURE. Translated from the 7th German edition. 150 illus. 254pp. 6⅛ x 9¼. T276 Paperbound **$2.00**

FOUNDATIONS OF MODERN ART, A. Ozenfant. Stimulating discussion of human creativity from paleolithic cave painting to modern painting, architecture, decorative arts. Fully illustrated with works of Gris, Lipchitz, Léger, Picasso, primitive, modern artifacts, architecture, industrial art, much more. 226 illustrations. 368pp. 6⅛ x 9¼. T215 Paperbound **$1.95**

HANDICRAFTS, APPLIED ART, ART SOURCES, ETC.

WILD FOWL DECOYS, J. Barber. The standard work on this fascinating branch of folk art, ranging from Indian mud and grass devices to realistic wooden decoys. Discusses styles, types, periods; gives full information on how to make decoys. 140 illustrations (including 14 new plates) show decoys and provide full sets of plans for handicrafters, artists, hunters, and students of folk art. 281pp. 7⅞ x 10¾. Deluxe edition. T11 Clothbound **$8.50**

METALWORK AND ENAMELLING, H. Maryon. Probably the best book ever written on the subject. Tells everything necessary for the home manufacture of jewelry, rings, ear pendants, bowls, etc. Covers materials, tools, soldering, filigree, setting stones, raising patterns, repoussé work, damascening, niello, cloisonné, polishing, assaying, casting, and dozens of other techniques. The best substitute for apprenticeship to a master metalworker. 363 photos and figures. 374pp. 5½ x 8½. T183 Clothbound **$7.50**

SHAKER FURNITURE, E. D. and F. Andrews. The most illuminating study of Shaker furniture ever written. Covers chronology, craftsmanship, houses, shops, etc. Includes over 200 photographs of chairs, tables, clocks, beds, benches, etc. "Mr. & Mrs. Andrews know all there is to know about Shaker furniture," Mark Van Doren, NATION. 48 full-page plates. 192pp. Deluxe cloth binding. 7⅞ x 10¾. T7 Clothbound **$6.00**

PRIMITIVE ART, Franz Boas. A great American anthropologist covers theory, technical virtuosity, styles, symbolism, patterns, etc. of primitive art. The more than 900 illustrations will interest artists, designers, craftworkers. Over 900 illustrations. 376pp. 5⅜ x 8.
T25 Paperbound **$1.95**

ON THE LAWS OF JAPANESE PAINTING, H. Bowie. The best possible substitute for lessons from an oriental master. Treats both spirit and technique; exercises for control of the brush; inks, brushes, colors; use of dots, lines to express whole moods, etc. 220 illus. 132pp. 6⅛ x 9¼. T30 Paperbound **$1.95**

HANDBOOK OF ORNAMENT, F. S. Meyer. One of the largest collections of copyright-free traditional art: over 3300 line cuts of Greek, Roman, Medieval, Renaissance, Baroque, 18th and 19th century art motifs (tracery, geometric elements, flower and animal motifs, etc.) and decorated objects (chairs, thrones, weapons, vases, jewelry, armor, etc.). Full text. 3300 illustrations. 562pp. 5⅜ x 8. T302 Paperbound **$2.00**

THREE CLASSICS OF ITALIAN CALLIGRAPHY. Oscar Ogg, ed. Exact reproductions of three famous Renaissance calligraphic works: Arrighi's OPERINA and IL MODO, Tagliente's LO PRESENTE LIBRO, and Palatino's LIBRO NUOVO. More than 200 complete alphabets, thousands of lettered specimens, in Papal Chancery and other beautiful, ornate handwriting. Introduction. 245 plates. 282pp. 6⅛ x 9¼. T212 Paperbound **$1.95**

THE HISTORY AND TECHNIQUES OF LETTERING, A. Nesbitt. A thorough history of lettering from the ancient Egyptians to the present, and a 65-page course in lettering for artists. Every major development in lettering history is illustrated by a complete alphabet. Fully analyzes such masters as Caslon, Koch, Garamont, Jenson, and many more. 89 alphabets, 165 other specimens. 317pp. 5⅜ x 8. T427 Paperbound **$2.00**

LETTERING AND ALPHABETS, J. A. Cavanagh. An unabridged reissue of "Lettering," containing the full discussion, analysis, illustration of 89 basic hand lettering tyles based on Caslon, Bodoni, Gothic, many other types. Hundreds of technical hints on construction, strokes, pens, brushes, etc. 89 alphabets, 72 lettered specimens, which may be reproduced permission-free. 121pp. 9¾ x 8. T53 Paperbound **$1.25**

THE HUMAN FIGURE IN MOTION, Eadweard Muybridge. The largest collection in print of Muybridge's famous high-speed action photos. 4789 photographs in more than 500 action-strip-sequences (at shutter speeds up to 1/6000th of a second) illustrate men, women, children—mostly undraped—performing such actions as walking, running, getting up, lying down, carrying objects, throwing, etc. "An unparalleled dictionary of action for all artists," AMERICAN ARTIST. 390 full-page plates, with 4789 photographs. Heavy glossy stock, reinforced binding with headbands. 7⅞ x 10¾. T204 Clothbound **$10.00**

ANIMALS IN MOTION, Eadweard Muybridge. The largest collection of animal action photos in print. 34 different animals (horses, mules, oxen, goats, camels, pigs, cats, lions, gnus, deer, monkeys, eagles—and 22 others) in 132 characteristic actions. All 3919 photographs are taken in series at speeds up to 1/1600th of a second, offering artists, biologists, cartoonists a remarkable opportunity to see exactly how an ostrich's head bobs when running, how a lion puts his foot down, how an elephant's knee bends, how a bird flaps his wings, thousands of other hard-to-catch details. "A really marvelous series of plates," NATURE. 380 full-pages of plates. Heavy glossy stock, reinforced binding with headbands. 7⅞ x 10¾. T203 Clothbound **$10.00**

THE BOOK OF SIGNS, R. Koch. 493 symbols—crosses, monograms, astrological, biological symbols, runes, etc.—from ancient manuscripts, cathedrals, coins, catacombs, pottery. May be reproduced permission-free. 493 illustrations by Fritz Kredel. 104pp. 6⅛ x 9¼. T162 Paperbound **$1.00**

A HANDBOOK OF EARLY ADVERTISING ART, C. P. Hornung. The largest collection of copyright-free early advertising art ever compiled. Vol. I: 2,000 illustrations of animals, old automobiles, buildings, allegorical figures, fire engines, Indians, ships, trains, more than 33 other categories! Vol II: Over 4,000 typographical specimens; 600 Roman, Gothic, Barnum, Old English faces; 630 ornamental type faces; hundreds of scrolls, initials, flourishes, etc. "A remarkable collection," PRINTERS' INK.

Vol. I: Pictorial Volume. Over 2000 illustrations. 256pp. 9 x 12. T122 Clothbound **$10.00**
Vol. II: Typographical Volume. Over 4000 speciments. 319pp. 9 x 12. T123 Clothbound **$10.00**
Two volume set, Clothbound, only **$18.50**

DESIGN FOR ARTISTS AND CRAFTSMEN, L. Wolchonok. The most thorough course on the creation of art motifs and designs. Shows you step-by-step, with hundreds of examples and 113 detailed exercises, how to create original designs from geometric patterns, plants, birds, animals, humans, and man-made objects. "A great contribution to the field of design and crafts," N. Y. SOCIETY OF CRAFTSMEN. More than 1300 entirely new illustrations. xv + 207pp. 7⅞ x 10¾. T274 Clothbound **$4.95**

HANDBOOK OF DESIGNS AND DEVICES, C. P. Hornung. A remarkable working collection of 1836 basic designs and variations, all copyright-free. Variations of circle, line, cross, diamond, swastika, star, scroll, shield, many more. Notes on symbolism. "A necessity to every 'designer who would be original without having to labor heavily," ARTIST and ADVERTISER. 204 plates. 240pp. 5⅜ x 8.

T125 Paperbound **$1.90**

THE UNIVERSAL PENMAN, George Bickham. Exact reproduction of beautiful 18th century book of handwriting. 22 complete alphabets in finest English roundhand, other scripts, over 2000 elaborate flourishes, 122 calligraphic illustrations, etc. Material is copyright-free. "An essential part of any art library, and a book of permanent value," AMERICAN ARTIST. 212 plates. 224pp. 9 x 13¾. T20 Clothbound **$10.00**

AN ATLAS OF ANATOMY FOR ARTISTS, F. Schider. This standard work contains 189 full-page plates, more than 647 illustrations of all aspects of the human skeleton, musculature, cutaway portions of the body, each part of the anatomy, hand forms, eyelids, breasts, location of muscles under the flesh, etc. 59 plates illustrate how Michelangelo, da Vinci, Goya, 15 others, drew human anatomy. New 3rd edition enlarged by 52 new illustrations by Cloquet, Barcsay. "The standard reference tool," AMERICAN LIBRARY ASSOCIATION. "Excellent," AMERICAN ARTIST. 189 plates, 647 illustrations. xxvi + 192pp. 7⅞ x 10⅝. T241 Clothbound **$6.00**

AN ATLAS OF ANIMAL ANATOMY FOR ARTISTS, W. Ellenberger, H. Baum, H. Dittrich. The largest, richest animal anatomy for artists in English. Form, musculature, tendons, bone structure, expression, detailed cross sections of head, other features, of the horse, lion, dog, cat, deer, seal, kangaroo, cow, bull, goat, monkey, hare, many other animals. "Highly recommended," DESIGN. Second, revised, enlarged edition with new plates from Cuvier, Stubbs, etc. 288 illustrations. 153pp. 11⅜ x 9. T82 Clothbound **$6.00**

ANIMAL DRAWING: ANATOMY AND ACTION FOR ARTISTS, C. R. Knight. 158 studies, with full accompanying text, of such animals as the gorilla, bear, bison, dromedary, camel, vulture, pelican, iguana, shark, etc., by one of the greatest modern masters of animal drawing. Innumerable tips on how to get life expression into your work. "An excellent reference work,' SAN FRANCISCO CHRONICLE. 158 illustrations. 156pp. 10½ x 8½.
T426 Paperbound **$2.00**

THE CRAFTSMAN'S HANDBOOK, Cennino Cennini. The finest English translation of IL LIBRO DELL' ARTE, the 15th century introduction to art technique that is both a mirror of Quatrocento life and a source of many useful but •nearly forgotten facets of the painter's art. 4 illustrations. xxvii + 142pp. D. V. Thompson, translator. 6⅛ x 9¼. T54 Paperbound **$1.50**

THE BROWN DECADES, Lewis Mumford. A picture of the "buried renaissance" of the post-Civil War period, and the founding of modern architecture (Sullivan, Richardson, Root, Roebling), landscape development (Marsh, Olmstead, Eliot), and the graphic arts (Homer, Eakins, Ryder). 2nd revised, enlarged edition. Bibliography. 12 illustrations. xiv + 266 pp. 5⅜ x 8. T200 Paperbound **$1.65**

STIEGEL GLASS, F. W. Hunter. The story of the most highly esteemed early American glassware, fully illustrated. How a German adventurer, "Baron" Stiegel, founded a glass empire; detailed accounts of individual glasswork. "This pioneer work is reprinted in an edition even more beautiful than the original," ANTIQUES DEALER. New introduction by Helen McKearin. 171 illustrations, 12 in full color. xxii + 338pp. 7⅞ x 10¾. T128 Clothbound **$10.00**

THE HUMAN FIGURE, J. H. Vanderpoel. Not just a picture book, but a complete course by a famous figure artist. Extensive text, illustrated by 430 pencil and charcoal drawings of both male and female anatomy. 2nd enlarged edition. Foreword. 430 illus. 143pp. 6⅛ x 9¼. T432 Paperbound **$1.45**

PINE FURNITURE OF EARLY NEW ENGLAND, R. H. Kettell. Over 400 illustrations, over 50 working drawings of early New England chairs, benches, beds cupboards, mirrors, shelves, tables, other furniture esteemed for simple beauty and character. "Rich store of illustra- tions . . . emphasizes the individuality and varied design," ANTIQUES. 413 illustrations, 55 working drawings. 475pp. 8 x 10¾. T145 Clothbound **$10.00**

BASIC BOOKBINDING, A. W. Lewis. Enables both beginners and experts to rebind old books or bind paperbacks in hard covers. Treats materials, tools; gives step-by-step instruction in how to collate a book, sew it back it, make boards, etc. 261 illus. Appendices. 155pp. 5⅜ x 8. T169 Paperbound **$1.35**

DESIGN MOTIFS OF ANCIENT MEXICO, J. Enciso. Nearly 90% of these 766 superb designs from Aztec, Olmec, Totonac, Maya, and Toltec origins are unobtainable elsewhere! Contains plumed serpents, wind gods, animals, demons, dancers, monsters, etc. Excellent applied design source. Originally $17.50. 766 illustrations, thousands of motifs. 192pp. 6⅛ x 9¼. T84 Paperbound **$1.85**

AFRICAN SCULPTURE, Ladislas Segy. 163 full-page plates illustrating masks, fertility figures, ceremonial objects, etc., of 50 West and Central African tribes—95% never before illustrated. 34-page introduction to African sculpture. "Mr. Segy is one of its top authorities," NEW YORKER. 164 full-page photographic plates. Introduction. Bibliography. 244pp. 6⅛ x 9¼. T396 Paperbound **$2.00**

THE PROCESSES OF GRAPHIC REPRODUCTION IN PRINTING, H. Curwen. A thorough and prac- tical survey of wood, linoleum, and rubber engraving; copper engraving; drypoint, mezzotint, etching, aquatint, steel engraving, die sinking, stencilling, lithography (extensively); photo- graphic reproduction utilizing line, continuous tone, photoengravure, collotype; every other process in general use. Note on color reproduction. Section on bookbinding. Over 200 illustra- tions, 25 in color. 143pp. 5½ x 8½. T512 Clothbound **$4.00**

CALLIGRAPHY, J. G. Schwandner. First reprinting in 200 years of this legendary book of beautiful handwriting. Over 300 ornamental initials, 12 complete calligraphic alphabets, over 150 ornate frames and panels, 75 calligraphic pictures of cherubs, stags, lions, etc., thou- sands of flourishes, scrolls, etc., by the greatest 18th century masters. All material can be copied or adapted without permission. Historical introduction. 158 full-page plates. 368pp. 9 x 13. T475 Clothbound **$10.00**

* * *

A DIDEROT PICTORIAL ENCYCLOPEDIA OF TRADES AND INDUSTRY, Manufacturing and the Technical Arts in Plates Selected from "L'Encyclopédie ou Dictionnaire Raisonné des Sciences, des Arts, et des Métiers," of Denis Diderot, edited with text by C. Gillispie. Over 2000 illustrations on 485 full-page plates. Magnificent 18th century engravings of men, women, and children working at such trades as milling flour, cheesemaking, charcoal burning, mining, silverplating, shoeing horses, making fine glass, printing, hundreds more, showing details of machinery, different steps in sequence, etc. A remarkable art work, but also the largest collection of working figures in print, copyright-free, for art directors, designers, etc. Two vols. 920pp. 9 x 12. Heavy library cloth. T421 Two volume set **$18.50**

* * *

SILK SCREEN TECHNIQUES, J. Biegeleisen, M. Cohn. A practical step-by-step home course in one of the most versatile, least expensive graphic arts processes. How to build an inexpensive silk screen, prepare stencils, print, achieve special textures, use color, etc. Every step explained, diagrammed. 149 illustrations, 8 in color. 201pp. 6⅛ x 9¼. T433 Paperbound **$1.45**

PUZZLES, GAMES, AND ENTERTAINMENTS

MATHEMATICS, MAGIC AND MYSTERY, Martin Gardner. Astonishing feats of mind reading, mystifying "magic" tricks, are often based on mathematical principles anyone can learn. This book shows you how to perform scores of tricks with cards, dice, coins, knots, numbers, etc., by using simple principles from set theory, theory of numbers, topology, other areas of mathematics, fascinating in themselves. No special knowledge required. 135 illus. 186pp. 5⅜ x 8.
T335 Paperbound **$1.00**

MATHEMATICAL PUZZLES FOR BEGINNERS AND ENTHUSIASTS, G. Mott-Smoth. Test your problem-solving techniques and powers of inference on 188 challenging, amusing puzzles based on algebra, dissection of plane figures, permutations, probabilities, etc. Appendix of primes, square roots, etc. 135 illus. 2nd revised edition. 248pp. 5⅜ x 8.
T198 Paperbound **$1.00**

LEARN CHESS FROM THE MASTERS, F. Reinfeld. Play 10 games against Marshall, Bronstein, Najdorf, other masters, and grade yourself on each move. Detailed annotations reveal principles of play, strategy, etc. as you proceed. An excellent way to get a real insight into the game. Formerly titled, "Chess by Yourself." 91 diagrams. vii + 144pp. 5⅜ x 8.
T362 Paperbound **$1.00**

REINFELD ON THE END GAME IN CHESS, F. Reinfeld. 62 end games of Alekhine, Tarrasch, Morphy, other masters, are carefully analyzed with emphasis on transition from middle game to end play. Tempo moves, queen endings, weak squares, other basic principles clearly illustrated. Excellent for understanding why some moves are weak or incorrect, how to avoid errors. Formerly titled, "Practical End-game Play." 62 diagrams. vi + 177pp. 5⅜ x 8.
T417 Paperbound **$1.25**

101 PUZZLES IN THOUGHT AND LOGIC, C. R. Wylie, Jr. Brand new puzzles you need no special knowledge to solve! Each one is a gem of ingenuity that will really challenge your problem-solving technique. Introduction with simplified explanation of scientic puzzle solving. 128pp. 5⅜ x 8.
T167 Paperbound **$1.00**

THE COMPLETE NONSENSE OF EDWARD LEAR. The only complete edition of this master of gentle madness at a popular price. The Dong with the Luminous Nose, The Jumblies, The Owl and the Pussycat, hundreds of other bits of wonderful nonsense. 214 limericks, 3 sets of Nonsense Botany, 5 Nonsense Alphabets, 546 fantastic drawings, much more. 320pp. 5⅜ x 8.
T167 Paperbound **$1.00**

28 SCIENCE FICTION STORIES OF H. G. WELLS. Two complete novels, "Men Like Gods" and "Star Begotten," plus 26 short stories by the master science-fiction writer of all time. Stories of space, time, future adventure that are among the all-time classics of science fiction. 928pp. 5⅜ x 8.
T265 Clothbound **$3.95**

SEVEN SCIENCE FICTION NOVELS, H. G. Wells. Unabridged texts of "The Time Machine," "The Island of Dr. Moreau," "First Men in the Moon," "The Invisible Man," "The War of the Worlds," "The Food of the Gods," "In the Days of the Comet." "One will have to go far to match this for entertainment, excitement, and sheer pleasure," N. Y. TIMES. 1015pp. 5⅜ x 8.
T264 Clothbound **$3.95**

MATHEMAGIC, MAGIC PUZZLES, AND GAMES WITH NUMBERS, R. V. Heath. More than 60 new puzzles and stunts based on number properties: multiplying large numbers mentally, finding the date of any day in the year, etc. Edited by J. S. Meyer. 76 illus. 129pp. 5⅜ x 8.
T110 Paperbound **$1.00**

FIVE ADVENTURE NOVELS OF H. RIDER HAGGARD. The master story-teller's five best tales of mystery and adventure set against authentic African backgrounds: "She," "King Solomon's Mines," "Allan Quatermain," "Allan's Wife," "Maiwa's Revenge." 821pp. 5⅜ x 8.
T108 Clothbound **$3.95**

WIN AT CHECKERS, M. Hopper. (Formerly "Checkers.") The former World's Unrestricted Checker Champion gives you valuable lessons in openings, traps, end games, ways to draw when you are behind, etc. More than 100 questions and answers anticipate your problems. Appendix. 75 problems diagrammed, solved. 79 figures. xi + 107pp. 5⅜ x 8.
T363 Paperbound **$1.00**

CRYPTOGRAPHY, L. D. Smith. Excellent introductory work on ciphers and their solution, history of secret writing, techniques, etc. Appendices on Japanese methods, the Baconian cipher, frequency tables. Bibliography. Over 150 problems, solutions. 160pp. 5⅜ x 8.
T247 Paperbound **$1.00**

CRYPTANALYSIS, H. F. Gaines. (Formerly, "Elementary Cryptanalysis.") The best book available on cryptograms and how to solve them. Contains all major techniques: substitution, transposition, mixed alphabets, multafid, Kasiski and Vignere methods, etc. Word frequency appendix. 167 problems, solutions. 173 figures. 236pp. 5⅜ x 8.
T97 Paperbound **$1.95**

FLATLAND, E. A. Abbot. The science-fiction classic of life in a 2-dimensional world that is considered a first-rate introduction to relativity and hyperspace, as well as a scathing satire on society, politics and religion. 7th edition. 16 illus. 128pp. 5⅜ x 8.
T1 Paperbound **$1.00**

DOVER BOOKS

HOW TO FORCE CHECKMATE, F. Reinfeld. (Formerly "Challenge to Chessplayers.") No board needed to sharpen your checkmate skill on 300 checkmate situations. Learn to plan up to 3 moves ahead and play a superior end game. 300 situations diagrammed; notes and full solutions. 111pp. 5⅜ x 8.   T439 Paperbound **$1.25**

MORPHY'S GAMES OF CHESS, P. W. Sergeant, ed. Play forcefully by following the techniques used by one of the greatest chess champions. 300 of Morphy's games carefully annotated to reveal principles. Bibliography. New introduction by F. Reinfeld. 235 diagrams. x + 352pp. 5⅜ x 8.   T386 Paperbound **$1.75**

MATHEMATICAL RECREATIONS, M. Kraitchik. Hundreds of unusual mathematical puzzlers and odd bypaths of math, elementary and advanced. Greek, Medieval, Arabic, Hindu problems; figurate numbers, Fermat numbers, primes; magic, Euler, Latin squares; fairy chess, latruncles, reversi, jinx, ruma, tetrachrome other positional and permutational games. Rigorous solutions. Revised second edition. 181 illus. 330pp. 5⅜ x 8.   T163 Paperbound **$1.75**

MATHEMATICAL EXCURSIONS, H. A. Merrill. Revealing stimulating insights into elementary math, not usually taught in school. 90 problems demonstrate Russian peasant multiplication, memory systems for pi, magic squares, dyadic systems, division by inspection, many more. Solutions to difficult problems. 50 illus. 5⅜ x 8.   T350 Paperbound **$1.00**

MAGIC TRICKS & CARD TRICKS, W. Jonson. Best introduction to tricks with coins, bills, eggs, ribbons, slates, cards, easily performed without elaborate equipment. Professional routines, tips on presentation, misdirection, etc. Two books bound as one: 52 tricks with cards, 37 tricks with common objects. 106 figures. 224pp. 5⅜ x 8.   T909 Paperbound **$1.00**

MATHEMATICAL PUZZLES OF SAM LOYD, selected and edited by M. Gardner. 177 most ingenious mathematical puzzles of America's greatest puzzle originator, based on arithmetic, algebra, game theory, dissection, route tracing, operations research, probability, etc. 120 drawings, diagrams. Solutions. 187pp. 5⅜ x 8.   T498 Paperbound **$1.00**

THE ART OF CHESS, J. Mason. The most famous general study of chess ever written. More than 90 openings, middle game, end game, how to attack, sacrifice, defend, exchange, form general strategy. Supplement on "How Do You Play Chess?" by F. Reinfeld. 448 diagrams. 356pp. 5⅜ x 8.   T463 Paperbound **$1.85**

HYPERMODERN CHESS as Developed in the Games of its Greatest Exponent, ARON NIMZOVICH, F. Reinfeld, ed. Learn how the game's greatest innovator defeated Alekhine, Lasker, and many others; and use these methods in your own game. 180 diagrams. 228pp. 5⅜ x 8.
T448 Paperbound **$1.35**

A TREASURY OF CHESS LORE, F. Reinfeld, ed. Hundreds of fascinating stories by and about the masters, accounts of tournaments and famous games, aphorisms, word portraits, little known incidents, photographs, etc., that will delight the chess enthusiast captivate the beginner. 49 photographs (14 full-page plates), 12 diagrams. 315pp. 5⅜ x 8.
T458 Paperbound **$1.75**

A NONSENSE ANTHOLOGY, collected by Carolyn Wells. 245 of the best nonsense verses ever written: nonsense puns, absurd arguments, mock epics, nonsense ballads, "sick" verses, dog-Latin verses, French nonsense verses, limericks. Lear, Carroll, Belloc, Burgess, nearly 100 other writers. Introduction by Carolyn Wells. 3 indices: Title, Author, First Lines. xxxiii + 279pp. 5⅜ x 8.   T499 Paperbound **$1.25**

SYMBOLIC LOGIC and THE GAME OF LOGIC, Lewis Carroll. Two delightful puzzle books by the author of "Alice," bound as one. Both works concern the symbolic representation of traditional logic and together contain more than 500 ingenious, amusing and instructive syllogistic puzzlers. Total of 326pp. 5⅜ x 8.   T492 Paperbound **$1.50**

PILLOW PROBLEMS and A TANGLED TALE, Lewis Carroll. Two of Carroll's rare puzzle works bound as one. "Pillow Problems" contain 72 original math puzzles. The puzzles in "A Tangled Tale" are given in delightful story form. Total of 291pp. 5⅜ x 8.   T493 Paperbound **$1.50**

PECK'S BAD BOY AND HIS PA, G. W. Peck. Both volumes of one of the most widely read of all American humor books. A classic of American folk humor, also invaluable as a portrait of an age. 100 original illustrations. Introduction by E. Bleiler. 347pp. 5⅜ x 8.
T497 Paperbound **$1.35**

Dover publishes books on art, music, philosophy, literature, languages, history, social sciences, psychology, handcrafts, orientalia, puzzles and entertainments, chess, pets and gardens, books explaining science, intermediate and higher mathematics mathematical physics, engineering, biological sciences, earth sciences, classics of science, etc. Write to:

Dept. catrr.
Dover Publications, Inc.
180 Varick Street, N. Y. 14, N. Y.